All the Above

My son's battle with brain cancer

Also by Julia McDermott:

MAKE THAT DEUX

UNDERWATER

All the Above

My son's battle with brain cancer

Julia McDermott (signature)

Julia McDermott

Cover art by Michael Faron

This is a work of creative nonfiction. The events are portrayed to
the best of the author's memory. While all the stories in this book
are true, some names and identifying details have been changed to
protect the privacy of the people involved, and some first names
have been changed to avoid confusion with other people of the
same name. The conversations in the book all come from the
author's recollections, though they are not written to represent
word-for-word transcripts. Rather, the author has retold them in a
way that evokes the feeling and meaning of what was said, and in
all instances, the essence of the dialogue is accurate.

ISBN–13: 978-1508624189
ISBN–10: 1508624186

Visit juliamcdermottbooks.com to order additional copies.

*For
my son, Jack,
my husband, Dennis,*

*and in memory of
my father,
Randy*

Just try (not all at once, just step by step)
to have hope. Resiliency is a wonderful thing.
Sometimes something great happens
when all feels lost.

— Jack McDermott

Chapter 1

May 8

"We must meet reverses boldly, and not suffer them
to frighten us, my dear. We must learn to act the play out.
We must live misfortune down, Trot!"

— Charles Dickens, *David Copperfield*

None of my four children ever called me Mama. My name is
Mom, not Mama or Mother. But for six months in 2010, I turned
into a mama bear.

This is my story, the way that I remember it, of when I went
through something that I never imagined I would. When I felt all
the feelings you feel when you think you're about to lose your
child, when your child's survival is the only thing that matters.
You go through the motions of daily life, but only because you're
forced to, because your whole self is wrapped up in getting your
child to survive this thing that you don't even want to think
about, that you're scared even to talk about. And you pray all the

time that it will just go away tomorrow morning, please, God? And then the nightmare will be over, and you can wake up and know that it didn't really happen.

But it did.

Before it happened, I was busy—with life. I was wrapping up an addition to our house and about to choose new furniture and fabrics. I was having fun decorating and customizing the extra space in the home where we planned to live for the rest of our lives. I was booking tickets for our summer trip to visit relatives from my husband's large family, and I was looking forward to see-ing everyone. I was hard at work on my second novel, and I was running our household.

With teenagers and young adult children, my mom-duties weren't hands-on anymore. I was more like an air traffic control-ler, overseeing their takeoffs and landings, and providing help when requested. My biggest concern was my youngest, fifteen-year-old Annette, who had just had an outpatient procedure. I was thankful that it had gone well, and glad she was at home taking it easy. I was thinking about her twenty-four-year-old brother Brian, too, who had recently come home and was deciding where to transfer for the fall semester. I was in touch with his twin brother Keegan, who lived up north. And I was looking forward to their brother Jack coming home from his freshman year of college for the summer.

My story began the day Jack turned nineteen: Saturday, May 8, 2010—well, it really began the week leading up to that date, but I didn't realize it, and I slept peacefully during that week.

He had taken his last final exam at the University of Georgia on Friday, May 7. A few days before, he had called me saying he wasn't able to see the words on the page. I was surprised: he had never had vision problems. He had spring allergies, though, and I assumed that he had used too many eye drops, stayed up too late studying, or both. Without another thought, I told him to "suck it up" and get through his exams, and that when he got home, I'd make him an appointment with our eye doctor, Kelly Barrows.

That Friday, I drove from Atlanta to Athens and arrived in the parking lot next to his dorm in the late afternoon. Ten minutes later, he had all of his stuff in the car. On the way home, he talked about how excited he was that we were all going out to Dave & Buster's the next night for his birthday. As I listened to his stories about classes and friends, my mind wandered to thoughts of his sister.

Annette had had a four-inch scaly patch on her upper abdomen that her doctor had been watching for months. It wasn't serious—cancer had been ruled out early—but it was worrisome because it had slowly spread. A lab report had diagnosed it as a rare condition with a complicated name: confluent and reticulated papillomatosis. Annette was more annoyed than troubled about it, and had faithfully applied one prescription cream after another. When they failed to clear it up, we scheduled the procedure with a plastic surgeon. She had spent the last couple of days on the couch, being careful not to lift anything, per doctors' orders. She was tapering off her pain medication and planned to go back to school on Monday.

I was relieved that we had finally had the issue resolved. If she was careful not to strain her core muscles over the next couple of weeks, a light, thin scar would replace the ugly raised brown patch on her skin. It wasn't a perfect solution, but it was the best one possible, and I trusted her doctor, known to be one of the best in his field.

When Jack and I arrived at the house on Friday evening, he greeted his father, my husband Dennis, who had just gotten home from work. Dennis and I sat down to have a drink before dinner, and Jack said he was going to his room to take a nap. He said he was beat, and that later, he would fix himself a sandwich for dinner.

My baby boy was back in the nest, and at that moment, all was right with the world.

The next day, he slept until noon. After he ate breakfast, he went to Target with Brian to get some things Brian wanted. I started the dishwasher, then put a load of laundry in the washing machine.

I had a busy but relatively normal week coming up. Our contractor was scheduled to finish the two additions to our home: we'd had our master bedroom enlarged and our back porch converted into a living area. I was looking forward to having more room, especially during our annual Christmas party and when the kids came home for breaks. Our upstairs carpet had been replaced last week, and the blinds and shutter man was coming to install new window treatments next Friday.

When the guys got home from Target, Jack sat down to watch TV in the den with Annette. I walked in to check on her.

"Mom, have you called Dr. Barrows for that eye appointment yet?" asked Jack.

"I'll call her on Monday morning." Standing several feet away, I glanced at him, then started. Something was wrong. "Jack, would you look straight at me?"

He turned and faced me.

I flinched, but caught myself. "I'm think I'm going to call her right now."

"Good. Maybe she can see me today."

Dr. Kelly Barrows was our friend and neighbor across the street. She had an office in her home and had seen all the members of our family who wore glasses or contacts. Her daughter Christina was a friend of Annette's. I walked into the kitchen and picked up my cell phone.

"Hi, Julie," Kelly said brightly.

I spoke quietly. "Hey, Kelly. Listen, I'm sorry to bother you today, but I'm afraid something's up with Jack's eyes."

"What's going on?"

"Well, he just looked at me from across the room. His eyes are crossed, and I don't think he knows it. He can't uncross them. When I picked him up from Athens yesterday, I didn't notice it."

Kelly's voice changed from lighthearted to concerned. "I'm at Walmart, but I'm going home right now. Can you send him over to my house in about fifteen minutes?"

"Sure." My mind began to race. *Were his eye muscles damaged? What had caused this?*

I forced myself to stay calm. No matter what it was, Kelly would find out, and she would fix it. That's what I told myself to believe, at least for the moment. This had to be a temporary issue, something unusual maybe, but something that would go away—hopefully on its own.

I walked over to Jack. "Dr. Barrows is on her way back from the store, and wants to see you when she gets home."

"Great." Jack was sprawled on a chair. "I'm sick of seeing double."

Seeing double? What was he talking about?

Fighting my feelings of alarm, I went to find Dennis in the room we used as a home office, stepped inside and shut the door. I told him what I'd seen when I looked at Jack's eyes, and reported my conversation with Kelly. Dennis walked into the den, asked Jack to look at him, then gave me a look.

"Is something wrong, Dad?"

He looked back at Jack. "No. Mom told me Dr. Barrows is going to give you an eye exam this afternoon when she gets back from the store." He turned to me. "Julie, let's go out to the front porch. We can watch for her and let Jack know when she gets home."

I pressed my lips together, nodded, and followed him out the front door. He closed it and inhaled deeply.

"This is *weird*," he said, a bewildered look on his face. He put his hand on his chin. "I'm glad Kelly can see him. I wonder what the hell it could be."

"Maybe it's what the boys had," I said. We'd always called the twins "the boys," even after the birth of our third son. As toddlers, Brian and Keegan had been diagnosed with esotropia, a cross-eyed condition that was corrected with glasses. If left untreated, permanent crossing would have been the result. Both had worn glasses for a few years, and the condition had been resolved.

"Maybe," he said. "But I don't remember that being as sudden as this."

"Me, neither. If it's not that, though, what could it be?"

"Maybe he's just overtired. But he slept in this morning, didn't he?"

I nodded. "He also told me he was seeing double."

"He did?"

At that moment, Kelly pulled into her driveway across the street. Dennis and I walked back to the den and sent Jack over. Then we went back out to the porch and sat down on two rocking chairs to wait.

Ten minutes later, Jack came out of the Barrows' front door and strode back across the street to our house. Kelly trailed him by twenty feet. Dennis and I stood.

"I'm glad that didn't take long," Jack said to Dennis and me, then walked in the house, untroubled.

Kelly climbed our front steps and stopped in front of us. She was trembling. "This isn't good," she said. "I'm so sorry, but what Jack has is serious."

"Oh, my God," I said, my eyes searching hers for understanding. "What do you mean?"

She grabbed the porch rail. "What he has can only be caused by one of three things. The first is extremely high blood pressure—which is why I didn't want to talk to you in front of him. I don't want to alarm him and potentially cause it to go up even more, if that's what it is."

"What are the other two things?" Dennis asked.

Kelly looked at both of us, her eyes showing fear. "It could be a symptom of meningitis—"

I shook my head. "He's had the vaccine."

"Or—it could be caused by a mass in his brain."

"A 'mass'?" said Dennis.

"A—a brain tumor."

No, it couldn't be. That was crazy. "Could it just be a muscular thing—a temporary problem with his eye muscles? Or could it be esotropia?" I asked.

Kelly shook her head slowly. "I'm so sorry. Jack needs to see an eye specialist right away, so he can get diagnosed and treated."

"What do you mean, 'treated?'" asked Dennis.

"First things first," she said. "I've already called Dr. Ben Sturdy, one of my colleagues, who's with Omni Eye Services. He's on call this weekend, and he's on his way over to his office. It's right around the corner. Do you know where the Peachtree-Dunwoody Medical Center is? The one with the green glass windows?"

We nodded. I felt like the ground had collapsed underneath me, and I was getting sucked into a pit of quicksand.

"Good," said Kelly. "Park in the garage and go up to the third floor. He'll meet you in the hall when you get off of the elevator. Would you like to follow me over there, or—would you like me to go with you? I can go with you—"

"No," said Dennis. "I know where the building is. Should we go right now?"

"Yes. But try not to upset Jack—it could be his blood pressure."

"Thanks, Kelly," I said. She gave me a hug, then left. Dennis and I went back to the den.

"Jack," said Dennis, his face calm. "Dr. Barrows said you need to see another eye doctor today. He's on his way to meet us in his office."

"Good," said Jack. "Let's go."

"*Now?*" asked Annette, turning toward me. "I thought we were going to watch a movie together. What if I need you?"

"I'm sorry, honey," I said. I touched her shoulder and leaned down to kiss her forehead. "Don't worry. Brian's here with you. He'll help you if you need him."

"But—"

"Try to rest," I said. "Remember the doctor said not to lift anything. We'll see you when we get back, okay?"

"Okay," she said weakly.

I went to get my purse. We were in crisis-mode now. During our years as parents, Dennis had been the go-to person for crises, and this time was no different. He was the oldest of nine and had seen his mother handle more than one serious health situation. Our implicit agreement to let him lead the way and do the talking gave me some momentary assurance.

Everything would be all right.

We got in the car and drove the two miles to the medical building in silence. Unspoken questions hung in the air as we got out of the car, walked inside, and took the elevator to the third floor. I've always disliked elevators, and this time, on a weekend in an unoccupied building, I felt trapped, like being in a deserted, locked warehouse.

Dressed in khaki shorts and a polo shirt, Dr. Ben Sturdy was waiting for us in the hall when the door opened. He stood some inches under six feet tall, looked about ten years older than Jack, and was trim and fit. He introduced himself and two other young men standing behind him, explaining that they were ophthalmology interns. Dennis threw me a quizzical, concerned look as the doctor unlocked the door to his office. I guessed what my husband was thinking: *Why had two interns been called in on a Saturday?*

Dr. Sturdy's demeanor was calm as he ushered us inside. He made small talk and soon commented on Jack's height–at six foot four, Jack was used to the icebreaker.

Then the doctor took his blood pressure. It was normal.

He began to describe the examinations he planned to do. "Do you mind if the interns watch?" he asked Jack.

"That's fine."

Over the next hour and a half, Dr. Sturdy performed a battery of eye tests as Dennis and I hovered quietly nearby. He started with the typical equipment, instructing the interns to look through the lenses after he did. Then he placed Jack in front of a big piece of equipment that would test his peripheral vision. For the next twenty minutes, Jack had to look at a small screen and watch a black object inside a white orb. Every time he saw a red dot pop up outside of it, he had to press a button.

Last, the doctor took Jack to another room and placed him in front of an apparatus that took photos of the backs of his eyes: his retinas and his optic discs, where the optic nerves met the eyes. Then he printed a sheet of paper showing two big, round, blotchy red images, and said they indicated damaged blood vessels under extreme pressure coming from behind Jack's eyes. He told us to go to the emergency room at Northside Hospital immediately, and to tell the ER doctor that Jack needed an MRI of the brain. Before sending us off, he jotted down his cell phone number on a scrap of paper, in case the ER needed to reach him.

As we walked to the car and drove the up the street to the hospital, everything began to sink in. Okay, Jack could have an MRI, but it would show that he was fine. They would treat him with some kind of drug, and we would go home–that was all I was willing to believe.

My mind simply was not open to anything else.

We parked in the lot and walked into the emergency room entrance. After a few minutes with a triage nurse at the same hospital where he was born exactly nineteen years earlier, Jack was admitted. Someone led us down a puke-green corridor and into a cramped, dim exam room where a narrow hospital bed took up most of the space. The walls were a dingy shade of gray, and the air smelled like a mixture of antiseptic, ammonia and stale, dried sweat.

Jack sat on the bed. "I hope this doesn't take too long. I'm looking forward to going out to dinner tonight."

Dennis threw me a glance, his ice blue eyes betraying apprehension. He stood beside the bed and next to a large steel apparatus anchored to the wall. I sat on a metal stool next to a counter cluttered with sharp medical instruments. Abruptly, a blonde middle-aged nurse wearing pastel patterned scrubs entered the room. She greeted us and took Jack's vital signs, all of which were normal. Several minutes later, an ER doctor entered the room and introduced himself as Dr. Hughes.

He walked right up to Jack and focused on his eyes. Then he looked over at me and Dennis. So far, no one had told Jack that his eyes were crossed. The doctor moved a pen from side to side and up and down in front of Jack's face, instructing him to follow it with his eyes while keeping his head straight.

We watched in silence. One of Jack's eyes seemed to follow the doctor's pen, but the other didn't.

"Hmm," the doctor said. "You say you've seen an ophthalmologist already today?"

"Yes," said Jack.

"He saw Dr. Sturdy at Omni Eye Services," I said. "I have his cell phone number." I produced the scrap of paper and gave it to the doctor. "He said Jack needed an MRI." *Just do that, fix Jack's eyes, and then let us out of here.*

The doctor gave me a look. "Well, that's to be determined. Did this Dr. Sturdy call us before you arrived?" He took the note from me and skimmed it.

"I don't think so," said Dennis. "I mean, he didn't say he was going to. He just sent us straight over here."

"Okay, we'll give him a call. Give me a few minutes. I'll be right back."

Once he left, Jack turned to me and his father. "I guess this is a dumb question, but what's an MRI?"

"It's a test," said Dennis. "I had one done on my knee a few years ago. It's a kind of x-ray. It doesn't hurt."

"Good. How long does it take?"

"I'm not sure," said Dennis.

Another nurse popped her head into the room. "Mrs. McDermott? I need to talk to you about the eye doctor. Come with me."

I followed her into the hallway. "Have you talked to him?"

"Not yet. The number he gave you isn't a local number. It doesn't have a 404 or a 770 prefix–"

"You can still call. It's his cell number. He's local–we just saw him."

She cocked her head. "Well, I don't know–"

Was she kidding? "Look," I said, annoyed, "let me get my phone. I'll call him *for* you."

"No, no, ma'am, that's not necessary. We can call."

My pulse quickened. "When? Please do it now, or I will."

"Don't get upset," she said, pursing her lips. "I'll find a phone we can use. Go back into the exam room with your son, and we'll be with you soon."

As I made my way back, I passed an unconscious patient being rolled away on a gurney, its wheels creaking. A short series of beeps emanated from around a corner and metallic clangs reverberated from down the hall. I shuddered. Memories flashed in my mind of the summer long ago when, as a teen, I had volunteered at a local hospital. I had liked math in school, but not science, so I'd ruled out going into medicine. My experience that summer served as proof that I'd made the right decision.

I opened the door to our exam room and walked in. "They're calling Dr. Sturdy now." I sat down. I would tell Dennis later about my conversation with the nurse.

"We should call home," said Dennis, letting out a deep breath. "I'll talk to Brian and tell him where we are. He can take care of Annette, don't you think, Julie?"

"Yeah."

He pulled out his cell. I listened as he briefly explained our situation to Brian and added that we would call back later.

After twenty more tense minutes, Dr. Hughes reentered the small space, which now felt like a holding cell that was getting smaller all the time.

"Okay, folks. I just talked to the ophthalmologist, and we agreed that Jack needs an MRI. The problem is, it's almost six o'clock on a Saturday, so we have to call in a tech. We're about to do that, but I don't know how long it's going to take before he gets here. So you'll have to wait a little while longer. I'm sorry."

Did this hospital really not have MRI technicians working on the weekend? Were we the only people who had ever come in on a Saturday with a similar situation?

"How long?" I asked.

He regarded me for a moment. "I'm not sure. When I find out, I'll let you know."

"Thank you," said Dennis. The doctor left us alone in the room.

Jack raised his eyebrows. "I hope they can get this thing done soon, and then we can go home. What a way to spend my birthday!"

I was grateful that he hadn't fully grasped the situation yet—ignorance was preferable to alarm. He wasn't the most naïve kid, but he was trusting and sincere, and young for his grade in school. I offered him a look of sympathy. This *was* a crappy way to spend his birthday. "At least the tech is on his way over."

The hour and a half before he arrived felt like twenty-four. We watched television in silence while vague hospital noises sounded intermittently in the background. Thoughts of what might lay ahead pinged in my head like bullets ricocheting in a steel drum. I forced myself not to consider what the MRI could indicate. My stomach felt like it was missing, as if it had decided to skip this whole scene and leave my body until everything was back to normal again.

Finally, a fifty-something man of average height and weight dressed in light blue scrubs entered the room.

"Hello, Jack," he said with a gentle smile. "I'm the technician who's going to do your MRI. My name's Marcus." His face displayed no sign of annoyance that he'd been called in to work on a weekend.

"Okay," said Jack. "I'm ready."

Marcus chuckled. "That's good. I know you've been waiting a long time." He nodded at me and Dennis. "Thanks for your patience this afternoon, folks."

Marcus explained to Jack what to expect during the MRI and how it would feel. An IV would be inserted into his arm and he would lie on a sliding table that would move him into a magnetic tunnel. It wouldn't touch him, but the procedure would be extremely loud, and it would last a long while. During it, Jack would need to keep his head perfectly still.

"Fine," said Jack. "Let's get it over with."

Marcus had him sign some authorization forms, then whisked him away on the rolling bed. Dennis and I stayed in the room to wait again. Once we were alone, I told him about the hallway nurse's resistance to calling Dr. Sturdy's "long distance" cell number, and my offer to do it for her.

"I'm glad Jack didn't hear that exchange," Dennis said.

"Me, too. I wouldn't have wanted him to see me so frustrated and anxious. Do you think we should call Brian again?"

"Let's wait—and let's not call any of our parents until we know more, okay?"

"I agree. Let's call when we know something."

We passed the time flipping television channels and hoping for good news that I was beginning to fear wouldn't come.

It was almost nine when Marcus brought Jack back. A tall, olive-skinned man with thick, dark hair entered the room right behind them. He was wearing a white lab coat.

"Hello, everyone," he said. "I'm Dr. Chris Tomaras. I'm a neurosurgeon."

The hairs on the back of my neck stood up, and reality engulfed me. *Neurosurgeon?*

He stepped over to the bed. "Hello, Jack. You did great on the MRI. I've just seen the scan, and—"

"'Scan?'" said Jack.

"The brain scan. The MRI scanned your brain and gave me an image of it. Your visit to the eye specialist earlier today showed there's been some damage to your optic discs, where the optic nerves meet the eyes. So we took a look to see what's going on in your brain, behind your eyes."

"Okay. What did you find out?"

Dr. Tomaras paused, glanced at me and Dennis, and then turned back to his patient. "You have a brain tumor."

Jack gasped. "You mean I have *cancer?*"

I grabbed his hand. "*No,*" I said firmly.

"No, no, no," said Dennis. "You don't have cancer—"

"You have a tumor," I said. I leaned toward him and spoke quickly. "But it's going to be like what my friend Susan's daugh-

24

ter Emily had. She had a brain tumor, but it was benign. It was inoperable, but it wasn't cancer." I didn't know this to be 100 percent true (or even close), but—in an effort to calm both of us down—it was what I was going to go with, for now.

I just wasn't willing to accept the possibility that Jack's situation could be anything worse.

Dr. Tomaras gave both Dennis and me a measured look, then slowly turned back to Jack. "Well, the thing is, we really don't know if it's cancer yet. We have to find out. We do know that your tumor is sitting deep in the middle of your brain, in the midline area, in what's called the pineal region, right behind your optic nerves. Because of it, you're experiencing hydrocephalus, which is causing the blurred and double vision."

"What's hydrocephalus?" asked Dennis.

The doctor turned to him. "It's a buildup of fluid in the ventricle. The brain has four ventricles. Jack's hydrocephalus is in his right ventricle. Normally, this fluid is continuously drained and expelled in the body. But because the skull is a hard container,"— he cupped his hands in the air around an imaginary brain—"when fluid builds up for whatever reason, there's nowhere for it to go, and it can cause serious problems."

"What can be done?" asked Dennis.

"We need to drain the fluid. We need to do it tonight. If we don't, Jack will experience brain damage, permanent loss of vision, or both."

A numbness overtook my body. I felt like I couldn't breathe. *My child will not become brain damaged or blind.*

"How do you drain this fluid?" said Dennis.

"We insert a ventriculoperitoneal shunt. A VP shunt. It's a small tube that runs from the right ventricle of the brain to the abdomen—"

"A *tube*? Outside of my body?" asked Jack, his eyes wide.

"No, no. Inside." The doctor motioned along the side of his own head and neck as he continued, "We place it just under the muscle, behind your ear and down one side of your neck, and all the way down to your abdomen."

"So you won't be able to see it? I don't understand."

"There will be a slight ridge running along your scalp, but your hair will cover it. You'll see it occasionally on your neck when you turn your head a certain way, but it won't bulge out. It will be hardly visible and will disappear into your abdomen, where the tube ends."

"What happens to the fluid when it gets to my abdomen?"

"It gets absorbed by the body and expelled in your urine. It won't cause you any problems."

"How long will the shunt stay in?" I asked. I was still holding Jack's hand.

The doctor turned to me. "For the rest of his life."

What was he talking about? I'd never heard of this, but realized in a flash that we had no choice. *Jack* had no choice.

The doctor turned back to his patient and continued speaking. "Don't worry, Jack. Lots of people have shunts placed, and live with them all their lives. Even babies have them placed. There's no reason you can't live a very long life with a shunt—into your eighties or nineties."

Jack looked at me and his dad, then back at the doctor. "Wait a minute," he said, holding up his other hand, his crossed eyes wide. "I have an idea! How about if I wear really strong glasses? I *promise* I'll wear them all the time—"

Dennis flashed me a look that was one part amused and one part bewildered. Jack's brothers had worn thick glasses when they were young and he was a toddler, following them everywhere; then one day, they didn't need them anymore.

"I wish it were that simple," said Dr. Tomaras, shaking his head gently. He threw a glance at Dennis and me, as if to gauge our expressions. "But I'm sorry. That's not going to fix the problem."

"When do I have to have this done? Can we do it on Monday? Today's my birthday, and we're going to Dave & Buster's tonight to celebrate."

The doctor's voice was soft. "I'm afraid you're not going to be able to. We can't wait until Monday. We have to do this tonight, so we can save your vision."

"We can't wait two more days? I've had this problem with my eyes all last week during exams."

"That's just it," I said, looking at Jack. The numbness faded slightly and turned into a glimmer of strength and resolve. Whatever had to be done, had to be done—and fast. "I'm sorry about your birthday, honey. But the thing is, you've already had your few days to wait, over this last week." My voice cracked and tears welled up in my eyes. Why hadn't I listened when Jack called saying he couldn't read? Why hadn't I at least told him to go to the clinic?

"Your mom is right," said the doctor. "You've already done your waiting. Now this is an emergency. If we don't do the surgery tonight, you'll be blind by Monday."

"*Blind?*" asked Jack, his long frame tense and rigid.

"Yes. But don't worry, that's not going to happen," Dr. Tomaras said in a reassuring tone. "We'll do it tonight, and then your eyes will start getting better almost immediately."

"Wait a minute. You're going to operate on my *brain?*"

"It's going to be okay," said Dr. Tomaras. "I promise. I do this kind of surgery all the time. It will probably take about an hour. You'll be asleep, and it won't even seem like a minute. When was the last time you ate or drank anything?"

Acceptance and resignation registered on Jack's face. "Not since right after I woke up today. A little after noon."

"That's right," I said to the doctor. My mind had now snapped to attention. "He got up around twelve. We went to the eye specialist about two-thirty. He hasn't had anything all afternoon—none of us have."

"Not even water?"

"No," said Jack.

"Good," said Dr. Tomaras, smiling. "I'll be back in a few minutes with some forms for you to sign, Jack. Then we can start getting you ready for surgery."

He left the exam room, and Dennis took his place by Jack's other side, across from me. Both of us held our youngest son's hands. I felt like we had fallen down into an abyss together, no light visible at the top.

"It's going to work out, Jack," said Dennis. I wondered what my husband was thinking, and thought I knew. He was scared. "You'll get through this, and then your eyes will get better, just like the doctor said."

"But what about the tumor, Dad?"

"We'll figure that out afterward, with the doctor," said Dennis. "Let's focus on the present. I just thought of something. Julie, do you have a number for the O'Barrs?"

Dr. Tom O'Barr was an internist, our family doctor, a neighbor and a family friend. Jack had grown up with his son Brendan; they had gone to elementary school together. Tom's wife Kathy was a retired anesthesiologist.

"I have Kathy's cell number."

"Let's call them and tell them what's going on. We can see if they know Dr. Tomaras, or anything about him."

"Good idea," I said, and reached for my phone. It was almost ten o'clock. I dialed Kathy's number and left a message describing what was happening and asking her to call me back.

We all stared at the TV again, the noise and images providing a much needed distraction.

Around ten-thirty, Dr. Tomaras reentered the room. "Okay, Jack. I need to go over the risks of the surgery with you. Don't be alarmed. I just have to make sure you know what they are." I braced myself and watched Jack's face as the doctor continued, "The risks are: bleeding, infection, swelling of the brain, a blood clot, leakage of fluid, or damage to brain tissue or intestines. But don't worry. The chance of any one of these occurring is very, very small. None have ever happened to any of my patients, and I've been doing this for quite some time."

"Good," said Jack.

"Someone will be in shortly to have you sign some authorization forms. Then I'll see you soon."

A few minutes later, another hospital worker walked in holding a clipboard. Jack signed consent forms for the surgery, scrawling his name on page after page.

Dennis pulled out his phone. "I'm going to call Brian back and let him know we won't be home for a while. I think I'll step out into the hallway."

I nodded.

Too soon, a couple other workers entered the exam room and said it was time. They rolled Jack down the hall and over to the operating room, and Dennis and I walked alongside of him and held his hands.

Just then my cell phone rang. It was Kathy O'Barr.

"I'm so glad you got the message," I said, shaking. I didn't feel able to explain. "Let me give the phone to Dennis."

Kathy spoke to him and then put Tom on the line. I listened as Dennis brought him up to date. "We're walking with him over to pre-op right now," he said, a nervous edge to his voice. "So, do you know this guy, Tomaras?"

For the next several seconds, I learned more from my husband's body language than I did from his words. His shoulders tensed and relaxed a little, and the tightness in his forehead melted a few degrees. In less than a minute, he hung up and we sat down beside Jack in a pre-op space where long, pale green curtains had been pulled around to enclose us.

"They know Dr. Tomaras," Dennis said. "Tom said he's fine, and that he does do this kind of thing all the time."

"I'm glad they called back, even though it's so late," I said.

"Me, too. They're up at their house at the lake. Jack, don't worry. Everything's going to be fine."

"Thanks for calling, Dad."

"No problem." Dennis smiled, a tender look on his face. "We'll get through this, okay? Mom and I will be there waiting for you when you wake up."

Dennis had been wearing his brave-dad face all afternoon, trying to help me and Jack stay calm. Now he looked as if he were just about out of strength-and-stability-fuel. I trusted him not to break, however. Not yet.

How could this be happening? Only twelve hours ago, the world had been normal. Now it was full of uncertainty and fear. My son was about to have a tube permanently inserted into his body leading from his brain to his abdomen so that he wouldn't go blind or suffer brain damage. My mind flashed to the pictures of Jack's retinas that Dr. Sturdy had shown us. No wonder he had sent us straight to the emergency room.

A few minutes later, another nurse appeared. "You can wait in the surgery waiting room," she said. "It's just down the hall, through that door." She nodded toward an exit sign. "Dr. Tomaras will come talk to you out there when it's over, in a little over an hour."

She started to wheel Jack away.

I squeezed his hand, and he squeezed mine back. "I love you, honey. See you soon." I leaned down and kissed his forehead, my eyes misty. The numb feeling was back now and my throat was tight. I swallowed.

"I love you, Jack," said Dennis.

"I love you too, Mom and Dad."

Then he was gone.

Dennis wiped away a tear and took my hand. We walked through the exit door and into a large, gloomy, empty waiting room filled with teal blue vinyl sofas and chairs. Exhausted, we sank down on a sofa.

"Julie, do you want to say a prayer together?"

I nodded and drew closer to him, waiting for him to speak. A moment later, he whispered the words on both our hearts.

"Dear Lord, please watch over Jack tonight, and over his doctors. Please let everything go okay. Please let them save his sight and don't let him incur any brain damage. And please guide us as we move forward together and as we try to help him. Lord, let Jack live."

Tears fell down my face. I leaned my head on Dennis' shoulder and tried to stifle a sob. Then I murmured an "amen," and he repeated it and put his arm around me.

I looked at his face. "Thank you," I whispered.

"I love you, Jule."

"I love you, too."

"We've gotta have faith tonight."

"I know."

He let out a sigh. "We should eat," he said, his eyes glassy. "I think there's a McDonald's open on the first floor."

"I'm not hungry."

"I'm not hungry, either, but still, we should eat. We need our strength. I'll go get us something, okay?"

I nodded. "Fish fillet, if they have it." When Dennis returned ten minutes later, I munched on my sandwich but couldn't eat even half of it.

Fear took hold of me. What if this surgery didn't go well? What if Jack still lost his vision? What if his tumor was malignant? What if he had cancer? Would he die?

No. My baby boy will not die.

* * *

NORTHSIDE HOSPITAL
EMERGENCY DEPARTMENT REPORT
PATIENT: MCDERMOTT, JOHN DENNIS
MAY 8, 2010
TIME SEEN: 5:40 PM
HISTORY OF PRESENT ILLNESS: This is a 19-year-old white male who complains of a six day history of blurred vision and side by side double vision. He just got home from college. His parents saw the crossed eyes and took him to a doctor in the neighborhood who took him to an ophthalmologist today, Dr. Sturdy, who examined him thoroughly.

Dr. Sturdy sent the patient here for further evaluation and hopefully to get an MRI. The patient has a slight, if any, headache but no fever. He is not treated for high blood pressure.

PAST MEDICAL HISTORY: Negative for hypertension. No history of any medical problems.

SOCIAL HISTORY: He is a college student at UGA. He does not smoke or drink or admit to it.

FAMILY HISTORY: Noncontributory.

VITAL SIGNS: Blood pressure 116/79. Pulse 87. Temperature is 98.

PATIENT STATUS: A pleasant male awake and alert in no obvious distress. Healthy.

EMERGENCY DEPARTMENT COURSE: The case was discussed with Dr. Sturdy over the phone. We decided to order an MRI of the brain with and without contrast. Time is 6:00 PM.

All the Above

DIAGNOSTIC STUDIES: MRI shows hydrocephalus. He has a mass lesion in the mid brain measuring 2.2 cm x 1.4 cm.

IMPRESSION: Solid and cystic pineal lesion at the level of the aqueduct extending into the inferior thalamus on the left and bilateral cerebral peduncles causing moderate hydrocephalus without mid line shift or downward herniation. Differential considerations include germinoma among others.

Dr. Tomaras is called. He is in route to see and admit to the hospital. He has asked me to give the patient Decadron 10 mg IV.

PLAN: The patient is admitted to the hospital in guarded condition.

Total time spent on this patient excluding procedures is greater than 31 minutes and is qualified as critical care time.

Chapter 2

May 9

"It's come at last," she thought, "the time when you can no longer stand between your children and heartache."

— Betty Smith, *A Tree Grows in Brooklyn*

A little after one in the morning, Dr. Tomaras walked over to us in the empty, bleak waiting room, its weak florescent lights casting a dim glow.

"Everything went well," he said, his voice steady and calm. "He's in Recovery and doing fine. The shunt placement went very well. He didn't even lose much blood."

"Thank God," I said. Relief flooded through me, but it was tempered by anxiety and despair. We'd made it through the first step, but the first step only.

"Thank you, Doctor," said Dennis.

"Now, about the tumor," said the doctor. "It's located in what's called the pineal region. The problem is going to be diagnosing it. My guess would be it's a germinoma, but that's just a guess. As I said, it's deep in the middle of his head, right behind his eyes. So, it's very hard to reach."

"What do we do?" asked Dennis.

"Well, first he's going to need a biopsy." The doctor lowered his voice and continued in a more reassuring tone, "Many times, these tumors are benign, but not always. Of course, you can get on the Internet and learn more, and I'm sure you will. But I wouldn't advise doing too much of that at this very early stage, before we know exactly what type of tumor it is. Reading about all the different kinds might be overwhelming."

Dennis brought us back on track. "Are you going to perform the biopsy?"

Dr. Tomaras shook his head. "Someone else will need to do it. But first, Jack has to heal from this procedure. He's got staples in his head right here"–he placed his hand on the right side of his head, near the front–"and in his abdomen, on the right. He'll come back to see me in about ten days and get the staples removed then. You'll get post-op instructions when he's released from the hospital."

"Will you advise us on the biopsy, and going forward?" asked Dennis.

"Yes. One thing at a time, though. I'm not saying we don't have a serious situation. We just don't know a whole lot yet."

I was still unable to speak. Maybe the situation would become less serious when we knew more. Whatever type of tumor it was, maybe it *was* benign, and nothing would need to be done about it. That was my hope, and I was going to nourish that hope as long as I could.

"Doctor," said Dennis, "how did Jack get this tumor? I mean, do we know how long he's had it, or what caused it?"

"That's really hard to say. If, as I suspect, it *is* a germinoma, also called a germ cell tumor, those are thought to originate in the embryo. During fetal development, cells that are called germ cells normally migrate to the gonads, and become either eggs or sperm. But sometimes, the theory is, for whatever reason, they don't move to the right place. They go somewhere else, like to the brain, and they can get trapped there and multiply."

Had something happened while I was pregnant with Jack? What had I done?

"So, Jack could have been born with this tumor?" I asked. Dennis took my hand.

"We don't know the answer to that—right now, we don't even know if it *is* a germ cell tumor. Even if that's the case, it's very hard to speculate about its origin. However, diagnosing it is absolutely essential to knowing how to treat it. As I said, it may be benign, but for now, we have to proceed as if it isn't. It may well be malignant. We just don't know at this point."

Dennis squeezed my hand. "I forgot to ask you something about the shunt. Will it mean Jack can't do sports anymore?"

Dr. Tomaras smiled and shook his head. "He can do everything but scuba dive."

I raised my eyebrows. How could that be? "You mean he can play contact sports? Like football and basketball?"

"Sure he can. Is he on a college team?"

"No," said Dennis. "He was on his high school football team, but now he just plays with friends—mostly basketball."

"He can keep doing it: that is, after he's recovered. Like I said, the only sport he can't do is scuba. Does he do that?"

"No," said Dennis. "I don't think he'll mind."

"Good," said the doctor. "Now, how far away do you live?"

"About a mile," said Dennis.

"Well, once Jack leaves the Recovery room, he'll be taken to a patient room. You can spend the night with him there. You may want run home and get anything you need, and pack a bag for him—clothes and toiletries."

36

"Now?" I said.

"Yes. Go now. Then you'll be back in his room before they bring him up. Just tell them you're his parents, and tell them to take you to his room."

We found our way out to the parking lot, almost deserted at this hour. I looked up at the black, cloudless sky as we trotted to the car, and an empty, hollow feeling settled within me. We arrived at home a few minutes later. Brian and Annette were asleep in their rooms and didn't stir. It took us less than twenty minutes to pack and return to the hospital parking lot, where the few cars sat in reserved spaces. We took the elevator up to Jack's floor and a nurse took us to the room that had been assigned to him. We plopped down on the small tan sofa by the window.

"You can turn this chair into a bed," said the nurse. "There are some sheets and blankets in the cabinets over the sink. Your son will be here soon."

My mind flashed to another night I had spent with Jack in a hospital almost four years earlier. It seemed like a lifetime ago. He'd had an emergency appendectomy at Scottish Rite, a children's hospital across the street—the same place where Annette had just had surgery. When they brought Jack to the room after his appendectomy, he'd been awake and cranky. I wondered if he would be the same this time.

I closed my eyes and tried to dispel the memory. No matter how Jack dealt with discomfort tonight, he was not going to lose his sight. He had come through the surgery well, and whatever he had to do next, he was going to need us. I had to get over my shock and fear and start to focus on how I could help him. I tried to relax and silently asked God to help me.

Just after two o'clock, the door opened and two nurses wheeled him in. With much effort and on the count of three, they moved him onto the bed. He didn't resist or even speak as they laid his head on the pillow. The whole right side had been shaved, and a big bandage had been placed over the front; on the other side of his head, his long curly brown hair remained, unruly as ever.

"Looks like they could have shaved his whole head," said one of the nurses apologetically. "I guess he'll want a haircut, to even things out, when he feels up to it. Would you like me to turn the light off?"

I nodded. The length of his hair was the least of his problems, but he did look funny. "Hey, Jack," I said softly.

"Mom, Dad," he mumbled. "Is it over?"

Dennis plopped into a chair next to the bed and took his hand. "Yeah, and you did great. Don't worry, Jack. I'm here, and your mom's here, and everything's gonna be okay."

"Mom, it's Mother's Day tomorrow. I was gonna get you a gift, but—"

"Don't worry about that, honey," I said, my voice breaking. I leaned over and took his other hand. "The best gift I could get is you being alive, and able to see. We're gonna be here with you all night, and stay with you until we go home. We'll celebrate Mother's Day and your birthday later." Tears were streaming down my face. I leaned down and kissed his cheek.

Exhausted, I settled down to try to sleep on the sofa. Dennis stayed in the chair, holding Jack's hand throughout the night.

* * *

Nurses entered the dark room at regular intervals over the next several hours to take Jack's vital signs, and Dennis and I dozed on and off. When a staff worker brought in his breakfast tray, Dennis went downstairs to get coffee for the two of us.

Jack was groggy at first, but soon began talking and eating cereal and eggs. His eyes were no longer crossed, though one didn't track exactly with the other. With Dennis' help, he made it to the bathroom and back, then laid back in bed to watch Sports Center on television.

"Hey, Mom, do you have my phone?"

I fetched it from my purse. "Here."

He took it and clicked away.

"Wow–I've got tons of birthday wishes on Facebook."

"You can read them?" asked Dennis.

"Yeah. I can see a lot better now."

"That's great," said Dennis, smiling.

There was a knock on the door. Dr. Tomaras entered and walked over to Jack. "How are you feeling?"

"Not too bad."

"Good." The doctor checked his bandage and then focused on his eyes. "How's your vision?"

"Better. Not back to normal, but I can read messages on my phone."

"That's great. Your eyesight should continue to improve throughout the day. The pressure is off now, and your eyes are starting the healing process."

Jack let out a deep sigh. "That's good news."

"It sure is. Depending on how things go, you might even go home today–later this afternoon." The doctor looked over to me and Dennis. "We'll make sure he's up and around and feeling good, of course. You'll get a call from my office to make an appointment to get the staples out."

"Thank you," said Dennis.

"Now," said Dr. Tomaras, turning back to his patient, "get up and walk when you can–have you already been up to go to the bathroom?"

"Yeah."

"Good. You can rest this afternoon, if you're tired."

"I'm pretty tired."

"Well, that's to be expected. You've been through a lot. We'll talk about what to do next when you come in to see me, okay?"

Jack nodded and the doctor left us to continue his rounds. The morning slipped by in the weird way it always does in hospitals. After Jack ate lunch, he wanted to take a nap.

Dennis turned to me. "Let's go downstairs and get a sandwich. He can sleep while we're gone." I still wasn't hungry, but I agreed.

Ten minutes later, we entered the hospital cafeteria, where nothing looked or smelled good. I walked around aimlessly, vetoing the salad bar and every dish sitting under heat lamps. Giving up, I chose a pre-made turkey sub wrapped in cellophane. I found Dennis waiting for me at a table for two against the wall, across from the registers.

"Jule," he said, "how are *you* doing?"

"I don't know. Not so great."

"Me, neither." He took a bite of his sandwich, his eyes beginning to brim with tears.

I felt a lump form in my throat and couldn't bring myself to eat. "Oh my God, Dennis."

"I know. But let's try to eat. *Eat, Santa, eat,*" he said, using a family expression we'd borrowed from a Christmas movie long ago, when Jack was a little boy.

I picked up my sub and forced a bite of the tasteless food, then sipped my Diet Coke.

"It's good that we'll probably get to take him home today," he said.

"Dennis, how is this happening? What's *gonna* happen? What are we gonna do?"

A tear began to stream down his face. He took a sip of his drink and looked into my eyes, his own watery and red. "I don't know, baby."

Tears began to fall down my cheeks and both of us wiped our faces with napkins. "After we eat, let's go for a walk outside," said Dennis. "We need to get a change of scenery—get out of here, and talk by ourselves."

"Okay."

We choked down our food and then trudged out of the hospital main entrance and under a bright, sunny sky. The outside world seemed unreal and unforgiving, as if it didn't care about us or what we were going through. We took a right and followed the sidewalk around the corner. Holding each other's hand tightly, we ambled toward a small garden area, found a bench, and sat down. No one else was around.

Dennis dropped his head and put it in his hands. "My God, Julie. Our boy has a brain tumor, and it may be malignant. He may have cancer."

Of the two of us, Dennis was the optimist, and I couldn't have him abandon that trait right now. "No. I'm not going to believe that. Not yet."

He looked up. "I guess we need to call Brian. And Keegan." Keegan was a seminarian studying in New England. Dennis pulled his phone out of his pocket, called home and brought Brian up to date. Then he called Keegan but had to leave a message for him to call us back. "Let's call my mom, then Randy and Sally, okay?"

Mary McDermott lived in Dallas; Dennis' father Jim had passed away two years earlier. My folks lived only a few miles down the road from us, and we saw them frequently.

I hesitated, then told him what I was thinking. "Go ahead and call your mom. I'll call Mom and Dad when you're done. But I'm not going to say Jack has a brain tumor."

"Why? What are you going to tell them?"

"I'll tell them about the surgery, and say it was an emergency. I'll explain that he had to have it because of a sudden vision problem."

"Don't you think they'll ask you what caused the vision problem?"

"I don't know, but if they do, I'll say we don't know everything yet. Which is true."

"Okay, but I think they're going to figure it out. You may regret not telling them what we know so far."

"I'm not sure they'll figure out he has a tumor. If they press me, I'm going to be vague. If I tell them about the tumor—well, I just can't deal with their reaction right now. They're going to be upset enough learning about the shunt. I'm still in shock myself. If they hear the words 'brain tumor,' they're both going to freak, and if they do, so will I."

He shook his head gently. "Okay. Do whatever you think is right."

"I know I'll have to tell them at some point. Just not today."

* * *

Dennis' mother Mary was a retired nurse, and she had an innate levelheadedness and a calm nature. After raising nine children, it took a lot to upset her. When he spoke with her and began to outline the course of events of the last twenty-four hours, she figured out from a medical standpoint that Jack had a brain tumor. Of course, she was shook up, but she didn't come apart, the way I feared my parents would. She listened to Dennis more than she talked; hearing his end of the conversation, I gathered that most of her questions were about the facts only. Before they hung up, Dennis told her that he would keep her updated.

I spoke to my parents afterward, and believed I was doing the right thing in not telling them everything. I felt good that at least one of our parents knew, though. My folks would find out the truth soon enough, and when they did, I'd be stronger emotionally, and more able to deal with their response.

However, I dreaded their reaction. I loved them dearly, but I knew them well. Like me, they were emotional, overly sensitive, and prone to worry; unlike me, they often had difficulty reining in their emotions. I wasn't great at that either, but over the years, I had absorbed some key methods from Dennis. My favorite way to handle difficult feelings was to delay my reaction. I was having a hard time doing that at the moment, and if I told them this afternoon that Jack had a brain tumor, I wouldn't be able to continue doing it. Telling them would push me over the edge.

Even though I had cried many tears over the last several hours, I'd been suppressing my feelings. I hadn't given in to panic and fear, and I didn't want to crumble now. Jack needed me to be strong.

Around four o'clock, he was released from the hospital. Dennis picked him and me up at the entrance, and five minutes later, he pulled the car up the circular drive in front of our house. The two of us helped Jack climb the eight steps to our front door and then walk to the den. He sat down across from the TV and put his feet on an ottoman and his head on a sofa pillow. Annette lay stretched out on the couch.

She grabbed my hand. "Mom, I'm so glad you're back!"

"How are you, sweetie?"

"Better, but not great. Why didn't you call me?"

"Dad called Brian—"

"You didn't talk to me."

"I'm sorry. I was going to call you, but when we found out Jack could come home today, we got busy and I forgot."

"How's Jack? Is he all right?"

"He's better, and he's okay for now."

"What do you mean, for now?"

"I'll explain later. Are you hungry?"

"Yeah," she said. "What's for dinner?"

"I'm not sure. Maybe we'll order a pizza." I went to the laundry room to put a load of clothes into the dryer, then back to the den and sat down in a chair to watch TV. Dennis was outside, putting in the tomato plants he had bought Saturday morning.

A little while later, he came in and walked into the room. "I'm going to get cleaned up and go to 5:30 mass."

"Okay," I said. "I'm not going. I'm staying here with Jack and Annette."

He nodded. "Julie, would you come upstairs with me for a minute?"

"Sure." I followed him to our bedroom.

We walked inside and he shut the door. "So how is he?"

"Okay, I guess." I plopped down on the bed. "I'm sure he's exhausted."

He sat down beside me. "Do you think it's sunk in?"

I sighed. "I dunno."

"I think we should sit down with Annette and Brian later tonight and explain things to them. Has Keegan called back?"

"Not yet. Let's talk to them after dinner. I thought I'd order pizza."

"Perfect," said Dennis. He put his arm around me. "I hope you don't mind that I went out to plant the tomatoes—"

"Of course not." I rested my head on his shoulder.

"I just needed to do something normal, you know? Something that would make me feel normal, at least. I needed to get those plants in the ground this weekend, anyway."

"I know."

"And you don't mind that I'm going to mass?"

"No, not at all." I reached for his hand. "You can pray for us."

"Yeah. I certainly will."

* * *

That night, the two of us helped Jack up the stairs to his bedroom, and I went down the hall to my room and changed into my
pajamas. Then I heard him calling me.

"Coming." I walked into his room, where he lay under the
covers of his queen-sized bed.

"Mom, can we talk for a little while before I go to sleep?"

"Sure, baby." I sat down on the edge of the bed. I was tired,
but I knew he had to be absolutely beat. "How do you feel?"

"Better. Not horrible, at least."

"You'll feel even better tomorrow. We can go get you a haircut—you need one."

"Yeah," he said, running his hand through the long curly
hair on the left side of his head. "But, Mom..."

I waited for him to continue, but he didn't. "What is it,
honey?"

He looked into my eyes, his own much straighter than I had
seen them earlier in the day, and I lifted a quick, silent prayer of
thanksgiving. Then his eyes widened, his eyebrows flew up and
his whole body stiffened. "It's this—this *tube*! I've got a tube in my
head now! And it's never coming out! Mom, what's going to happen to me?" His eyes filled with tears.

"Look," I said, taking his other hand and looking straight
into his eyes. My heart was breaking, but not about the shunt. I'd
gotten over it, and he had to, too. "Yeah, you're right. You've got
that tube, that shunt, in your head. And it's not coming out. It's
there for a reason, and you need it."

"Ugh! God! I feel like a freak!"

"You're *not* a freak. It's a shunt, that's all, and it's hidden in
your body. No one can even tell it's there."

"Oh, yeah? Look at this bump! You can see it–I can feel it, and I saw it in the mirror!"

"Your hair's gonna grow back, and it'll cover it, I promise. The bump isn't on your forehead, anyway–it's on your head, way up here." I pointed. "It's not going to bother you. The doctor even told us you can do every sport except scuba dive."

"He did?"

"Yes."

"Why can't I scuba dive?"

"I don't know–it must have to do with water pressure or something. But you've never scuba dived, and you've never said you wanted to. So what if you can't do it now? Don't worry about it. You gotta get better from this surgery, but soon you'll feel fine again. And you can see!"

"Oh, Mom. Why did this happen to me? Why do I have a *brain tumor?*"

I inhaled and let out a deep breath. Every bit of me was struggling to keep it together. I could *not* cry. "Jack. You may have had the tumor all your life–or you may not have. The doctor said we just don't know. But here's the thing: We don't *know* why you have it, and we're not going to know. So we're not going to ask that question, okay? Because asking that question is not going to help us. It's just going to take away our energy. And we need all our energy to get you well."

"But–"

"I know what you're saying. Really, I do. But I think we should decide together, right now, that we're not going to ask why. We could drive ourselves crazy if we do. The thing is, you have the tumor, and we're going to fix it–we're going to do whatever we have to do. And we're not taking 'no' for an answer. Okay?"

"What are we gonna have to do?"

"I don't know yet. But we'll find out. This is going to be okay. We're not going to let it *not* be okay. Like I said, we're not taking 'no' for an answer! Got it?"

He nodded slowly. "All right. I just feel so *weird.* I can't believe this is happening."

"I know. Me, too. But it is, and we're with you. Me and Dad. Okay? Every day."

"Have you told Brian and Annette everything?"

"Yeah. We told Keegan when he called. Dad told his mom too, and he asked her to tell your McDermott aunts and uncles. But he told her not to tell any of your cousins—the younger generation." Our sixteen nieces and nephews on Dennis' side of the family ranged in age from twelve to twenty-four.

"Good," said Jack. "I don't want to talk to anyone in the family right now. I just wanna talk to you and Dad."

"I understand."

"Did you tell Grandma and Granddad? Or Aunt Pam and Uncle Bart?"

My sister lived in Colorado, and my brother lived here in town. "I called my parents, but I only told them that you had to have the shunt surgery to fix a vision problem. They'll tell Pam and Bart. I didn't tell them about the tumor, though. I didn't think I could handle their reaction yet. I hope you don't mind."

He looked relieved, as if he felt the same apprehension about telling them that I did. "No, I don't. Actually, I'm glad. I know we have to tell them sometime, but if you had, I think they would be calling and wanting to talk to me tonight."

"Probably. They love you, Jack, but I'm not sure they'd understand that what you need now is *not* to talk to them—that you need some time."

I knew my parents would call me again and ask more about what was going on, and that I could go on being vague for only so long. Once I told them about the tumor, it would be real—and reality was not something I felt prepared to embrace at the moment.

"What about Grandma Mary? Does she understand?"

"Well, you know how different she is from Granddad and Grandma Sally. Dad talked to her, but she understood. I know she's thinking about you, and she's worried, too. But she knows we need to digest everything."

"Okay."

"Jack, don't worry. We're gonna figure this thing out."

He looked at me for a second. "I love you, Mom."

"I love you, too. Now, let's get some sleep, okay? You've got to be tired."

"All right." He lay his head down on the pillow.

I leaned over and kissed his forehead. "We'll go get you a haircut tomorrow and go to Waffle House for breakfast, okay?"

"Good."

"Remember, me and Dad are right here if you need us. Goodnight, sweetie."

"Goodnight."

Five minutes later, I lay on my own bed under the covers next to Dennis, and I didn't hold back my tears.

* * *

OPERATIVE NOTE

MAY 9, 2010

PREOPERATIVE DIAGNOSIS: Pineal region mass with obstructive hydrocephalus.

POSTOPERATIVE DIAGNOSIS: Pineal region mass with obstructive hydrocephalus.

PROCEDURE: Placement of right Delta 1 nonprogrammable ventriculoperitoneal shunt.

SURGEON: Christopher Tomaras, M.D.

ASSISTANT: John Dobrasz, P.A.

ANESTHESIA: General endotracheal

ESTIMATED BLOOD LOSS: Less than 30 mL.

COMPLICATIONS: None.

INDICATION: The patient is a 19-year-old gentleman with a history of sixth nerve palsy and papilledema with progressive loss of vision. He was evaluated with an MRI, which showed a pineal region mass compromising the Sylvian aqueduct. After informed consent was obtained and he understood all of the potential risks of the surgery, he was brought to the operating room for placement of a ventriculoperitoneal shunt and sampling of the CSF.

HOSPITAL COURSE: Post-op day one, the patient's vision was much improved, incisional discomfort as expected, and tolerating regular diet, ambulating without complication or difficulty at this time, deemed stable for transfer to home.

DISCHARGE MEDICATIONS: Lortab as needed for pain. Avoid aspirin and blood-thinning products.

DISCHARGE INSTRUCTIONS: Activity encouraged. Avoid any straining-type activities. Keep incision dry. Call with any questions or should he have symptoms at any time.

NORTHSIDE - LAB - PATHOLOGY

CYTOLOGY REPORT

CEREBROSPINAL FLUID: HYPOCELLULAR SAMPLE; NO MALIGNANT CELLS IDENTIFIED.

CLINICAL HISTORY: Brain tumor; eye pain.

Chapter 3

May 10 - 18

Hope is a good breakfast, but it is a bad supper.

– Francis Bacon

I had just finished my first cup of coffee when Jack entered the den to find me watching the news.

"How are you feeling?" I asked.

"Better, but kinda weak. Can we go to Waffle House?"

"Sure. Do you want to take a shower and go get your hair evened out first?"

"I'm gonna shower, but I wanna eat before the haircut."

"Really? You don't care about going out in public with one whole side so much longer?"

"Nah. I need food."

I smiled. "Okay. I'll get ready while you're in the shower. Remember not to let your bandage get wet."

He ambled away to climb back upstairs, and I went to my room and threw on some clothes. Ten minutes later, we were in the car and on our way.

We walked into our favorite Waffle House, the one located halfway between our house and our kids' high school, and sat down in a booth. The scent of hot cooking oil, hash browns, and scrambled eggs wafted through the air. A hodgepodge of customers young and old dotted the counter seats and the other booths lining the large windows. A very short, blonde forty-something waitress in a yellow polyester uniform came over to our table.

"Hi there," she said brightly. "Coffee?"

Both of us nodded.

She returned a moment later and poured Jack's cup first.

"How are you today?" he asked her.

"Oh, I'm fine. How *you* doin'?" She looked at Jack's bandage. "Just get outa the hospital, honey?"

"Yeah." Jack smiled. "My name's Jack."

She grinned, poured coffee into my cup, and dropped some individual creamer containers on the table. "Mine's Rhonda." She pointed to her name tag. "Feel like a big breakfast this mornin', Jack? What can I getcha?"

"Let me have a waffle, two eggs over medium, white toast, and grits. No bacon or sausage. And a glass of milk."

She scribbled on her pad and turned to me. "And you?"

"I'll have scrambled eggs, raisin toast and grits."

"All right." She smiled at Jack again. "You been in a wreck, hon?"

He made a what're-ya-gonna-do face, his eyebrows raised. "No. I had surgery. I have a brain tumor."

She took a small step back, and a heartfelt look of compassion came over her face. Evidently, though he wasn't ready to tell our entire family, he didn't mind telling a stranger. Maybe it was a way to test the waters; the risk was smaller with someone he didn't know.

"Oh, no, sweetie! Well, bless your heart! Let us get your breakfast ready, and I'll get it right out for ya, okay, darlin'?"

"Okay." Jack gave her another smile. She trotted toward the cooks. He looked at me as he lifted his cup. "*She* was nice."

"Yeah, she was. She was kind." I glanced at her, wondering how many other young men she had served who were banged up with stitches and big bandages on their bodies.

"So how do you really feel today?" I asked. "Have you thought more about what we talked about last night?"

He nodded. "You're right, Mom. I can't know why this happened, but I'm going to do whatever I have to do. And I'm gonna try not to think about it."

I reached over and grabbed his hand. "Honey, I know it's a lot. The thing is, your whole world can change in one day. In *one day*. And ours did."

"*That's* the truth." His eyes fell.

"So now, this is our world. We have to deal with it. But it's gonna be okay."

"I'm glad I have that acting internship starting in a couple weeks. It'll keep me busy, and it'll help me focus on other stuff."

"When does it start again?"

"Monday, May twenty-fourth. It goes on for five weeks."

"And it's mornings only?"

"Nine to one. Shouldn't be too hard, and should be a lot of fun. I have to drive down to Decatur every day, though."

"Well, today's the tenth. That appointment with Dr. Tomaras will be sometime next week. I'm sure it won't be a problem for you to start on the twenty-fourth, but we can ask him if it's okay."

"Why wouldn't it be okay?"

"I don't know. I bet it'll be fine. You're not supposed to drive yet, though–"

"But by then, I'll be able to."

"I'm sure the doctor will say you can."

But if he did, I'd be visualizing my boy driving around town with a brain tumor sitting behind his eyes. What if something happened to him? What if he had a seizure?

"Plus, I'm supposed to volunteer for the first time at Whole World Theatre in Midtown on Saturday night, the twenty-second."

I had forgotten about that. Jack had been in an improv group at UGA, and a few weeks ago, he had contacted the theatre to ask if he could help out over the summer. They'd told him they would put him on the schedule a couple of times a week to work the camera and to take tickets for the evening shows. "That's after the doctor appointment. Let's mention it to him then."

Rhonda arrived with our breakfast. "Here you go," she said to Jack. "More coffee?" she asked me.

I nodded and smiled at her. "Thanks, Rhonda." After she scurried off, I looked at Jack. "I'm sure he'll say it's okay. Let's not worry about it."

"No, let's not."

"I'm glad you're feeling better."

"Mom, I feel so much better than I did yesterday. But I don't feel back to normal."

"Well, you won't for a little while. Remember when you had the appendectomy, and what I said about how you would feel after that?"

"Kind of."

"Okay. The first day, it's this." I put my hand in the air, level with my chin, my palm flat and facing down. "The next day, this." I raised my hand a notch, now eye-level. "Then, this." My hand was now level with the top of my head. "It's like stair-steps. Each day is better than the day before."

"Yeah, I remember, it *is* kind of like that."

"By next week, you'll feel much, much better." I looked into his eyes. One was slightly off, but nothing like what it had been previously. "I can't wait to get your hair evened out."

"You mean, shaved."

I smiled. "It'll grow back fast."

"Maybe we can go to Dave & Buster's this coming Saturday night. What do you think?"

"Sure. That's a great idea."

It didn't take long for us to finish our meal and pay the check. I gave Rhonda a big tip and thanked her again.

"You're welcome. You take care, now, Jack, okay?"

"I will, thanks."

Ten minutes later, we walked into an empty Great Clips and Jack sat down in a chair. The barber had a similar reaction to Rhonda's, spoke kindly to Jack, and was very careful to avoid touching his bandage. When he was finished, Jack's hair was close-cropped all over. He looked like a Marine who had just returned from battle with a severe head injury.

"If you wanna come back later this week, or after you get that bandage off, and you want me to recut it, come on in," said the barber. "No charge."

I went to pay the bill at the counter.

"No, ma'am," he said. "No charge for today, either."

I cocked my head. "Let me pay you."

"No, that's okay."

"Well, let me tip you then."

He held up his palm, facing me, as a "stop."

"Come on," I said. I handed him a twenty.

He smiled, took it, and said goodbye, and Jack and I walked out the door and went home.

* * *

That evening after dinner, Jack handed me a folded piece of paper. "It's your Mother's Day gift. I'm sorry it's late."

"Oh, sweetie, you didn't have to give me anything. Like I said before—"

"Just read it," he said. "It's not much. I just wanted to do something, and tell you how I feel."

I opened the sheet of computer paper that he had printed using our kitchen computer and printer. The words "Mother's Day Poem" were centered at the top, and his signature in pen was at the bottom. I was overwhelmed with emotion. For years, I'd written and printed birthday poems to all my kids, but no one had ever done one for me. Tears welled in my eyes as I read the lines:

The school year began, her son going off to school
She was afraid he wouldn't come home, he would be too cool
But she kept being a supermom, balancing kid's needs
While working on books for publishers to read

So fall turned to winter, and winter to spring
She got the house remodeled, because of "Cha-ching"
To Puerto Rico and Vegas, she went with Dad
Though her son was away, she wasn't sad

Then tons of things took place at once
Her youngest son came home: "I can't see!" he grunts
But she handled it all like a champ always should
But got shafted on Mother's Day, so this poem's pretty good

I looked up at Jack. "Thank you! This is so sweet!"

"You're welcome. Like I said, though, it isn't much."

"Oh, yes, it is! You took the time to do this, with the way you're feeling right now, with your eyes, and after what you've been through–"

"Really, Mom, it was nothing. I just wanted to do something for you. I love you. Happy Mother's Day."

"I love you, too. This is perfect. I'm going to frame it and put it right next to my computer!"

* * *

Later that week, I spoke to my parents on the phone a few times and told them Jack's sight was much better and that he was doing fine. I fielded their questions as best I could, and my explanations satisfied them to a degree. They kept pressing me with direct questions about the cause of his vision issues, and challenged me about why I wasn't more upfront with information. I was sure they suspected something else was going on.

They said they'd told Pam and Bart about the shunt surgery, but neither of my siblings had called. I wondered if either had speculated about why the shunt had been necessary, in their conversations with our parents. Perhaps, like my mother-in-law, they had figured out that Jack had a brain tumor. I felt guilty for not having shared the truth, but I reassured myself that if they knew why–*when* they knew why–they'd understand. At least, I hoped that they would.

Whether they understood or not, Jack's wish to keep mum was my priority, and keeping mum was working for me, too. I didn't know whether their feelings would be bruised, but in my mind, Jack's took much higher precedence. He had to face whatever lay ahead, and I thought he had the right to drive the flow of information, especially initially, as everything started to sink in.

Dennis agreed with me. If keeping quiet for the moment was helping Jack, so be it.

The knowledge that he had a tumor in his brain–and that he could have cancer–was an overwhelming burden, and I didn't want anything or anyone to add to that burden.

I was a mama bear now, and I was going to protect him as long as I could.

He had tapered off his pain meds with no problem, was eating well, and was up and around when he wasn't taking a nap. On Wednesday evening, he came downstairs and said his digestion had slowed to a standstill, and he was beginning to feel very uncomfortable.

"Mom, can you call the doctor and see if there's something I can take?"

"Sure. But before I call Dr. Tomaras, I think I should text the O'Barrs and ask if they can recommend anything over-the-counter."

"Good."

Kathy O'Barr called me back with some suggestions, and I went to the store. "Here you go," I told Jack when I returned. "This should help."

That night, we talked in his room again before he went to sleep, something we'd been doing every night since Sunday.

"How are you feeling, honey?"

"Okay. Still not normal, though." He made a face. "If only my system would work."

"I know. I'm sorry. It'll get better soon, though."

"I hope so."

I paused for a second. "Listen, I need to ask you something."

"What?"

"Well, I know you don't want to tell anyone else in the family what's going on yet, but do you mind if, sometime soon, I tell two of my very close friends, and tell them not to tell anyone?"

"Why?"

"Because I just—I need to tell somebody. Somebody that I know cares about me, and about you. At some point—but not until you're ready—we need tell all the family members. I don't want to rush you to do that, but if I could talk to two of my good friends now, I'd feel a little better, even a little stronger. They won't call you or ask you any questions. I'll explain to them how you're feeling."

"I guess that's okay. Who, though?"

"My friend Susan. I've known her for over twenty years. She's a cancer survivor. I think I told you, her daughter Emily had a brain tumor."

"All right. But who else?"

"Elen." Jack knew that she was one of my closest friends.

"Okay. But I don't want to talk to anyone except you, Dad, and the doctors."

"I understand. I don't blame you, honey. One more thing. Can my friends tell their husbands?" Dennis and I told each other just about everything.

"Fine."

Had Jack been a lot younger, or even still in high school, I might have prodded him harder to allow me to put the word out to family and friends. But he was nineteen and a legal adult, with almost all of an adult's rights and responsibilities. He was the one who had to sign the consent for surgery; Dennis and I couldn't do it for him. Given Jack's need for privacy—and his fragile emotional state—I felt selfish for asking him to let me confide in anyone, especially since we hadn't even told my parents. I didn't know if he really understood why I wanted to tell my friends, but I was grateful he didn't mind.

* * *

The next day, I met Elen for lunch at a nearby Irish pub, the Bat & Ball. I'd already told her that Jack had had emergency surgery, and said I would tell her the whole story when we met.

We greeted each other, sat down in a dark wooden booth in the back, and gave the waiter our orders. When he disappeared, she asked, "What happened? Is Jack all right?"

"Oh, God, Elen."

"What is it?" Her eyes were wide.

I swallowed. "He has a brain tumor."

"What? Oh, God! Julie! Oh, my God, I'm so sorry!" She reached across the table and grabbed my hand. Tears began to stream down my face.

Elen's son Andrew was a year older than Jack, and her daughters were one and two years younger than Annette. Although our kids had gone to different high schools and didn't know each other very well, she and I had shared a lot about them over the years.

"What happened?" she asked.

I wiped my face with a napkin and recounted the tale of the past weekend, pausing now and then to collect myself. Finishing the story, I added, "The doctor said it could be benign."

"Yes! It has to be benign."

"Elen, I don't know what I'm going to do if it isn't."

The waiter appeared with our lunch, set our plates in front of us, and then quietly walked away.

Elen spoke softly. "When will you know?"

"I don't know. First, he has to have a biopsy–that could show that it's benign. Like Susan's daughter Emily's. At least, I think hers is."

"Emily has a brain tumor?"

"She did–I think she still does. Susan told me about it several years ago, but said that it was inoperable. She said they went to M.D. Anderson, but all they've had to do is watch it. She's okay now, as far as I know."

"I had no idea! How old was she when they found it?"

"She was in middle school."

"Have you told Susan about Jack?"

"No. I'm going to call her later today, but Jack doesn't want us to let anybody else know yet."

"Does he mind if I tell Mark?"

"No. But that's it, okay?"

"Of course. Have you told everyone in your families?"

"We told Dennis' mom, but he told her to make sure no one tells Jack's cousins. We told my parents, but only about the emergency surgery. We haven't told them about the tumor yet. I feel bad about it, but we want to wait until we know more before we do. Jack's still in shock, anyway, and so are we."

"Oh, God, I'm sure you are." Elen took a sip of ice water, and then cocked her head. "You know, Julie, I don't blame you guys at all for not putting the word out right now."

"You don't?"

"No. I mean, this thing *just* happened. Here's Jack, just got home from his freshman year of college, and now all of a sudden, he has surgery, and finds out he has a brain tumor! I think he should take all the time he needs before telling the whole world—and so should you and Dennis."

"We're going to, sometime, though. And when we do—"

"Don't worry about that right now. Just take things one step at a time."

I inhaled deeply and let out a breath. "Oh my God, Elen. My baby has a *brain* tumor!" My tears began to flow again. "It's *got* to be benign—I just can't believe it isn't!"

She reached across the table and grabbed my hand. "Yes. It's got to be."

"My baby boy *cannot* have cancer!"

* * *

Later that day, I called Susan.

We had met a few years before Jack was born, right after her cancer diagnosis. Emily, Brian, and Keegan had played together as toddlers, and we became friends. In recent years, we'd attended the same Bible study group. Though I hadn't been a regular at meetings lately, I felt accepted and supported by the network of about a dozen women. Most of us went to the same church, and a few of the members were longtime friends.

Susan also understood why we hadn't put the word out to the community yet. "Jack's the one going through this, and he has the right to decide who should know about it, and when," she said.

"That's exactly how Dennis and I feel."

"But, Julie, I think he'll want you to tell people at church at some point. And when you do, the response from the community is going to be overwhelming."

"Really?" We'd been members of our parish for many years and knew lots of people through it and the parish school, which all our kids attended. Though I wanted the support of our community, an overwhelming response was exactly what Jack *didn't* want, and it was something I wanted to protect him from, until he was ready.

"Yes. But listen," continued Susan, "you're going to have to brace yourself. Sometimes, without meaning to, people will say things that won't be what you need to hear, and that won't be helpful. They'll mean well, but—without meaning to, some people might dismiss what you're going through. Or they may just not know what to say. You have to prepare yourself, and don't let it bother you if that happens. It doesn't mean they don't care."

"Oh, Susan—"

"And listen: some people will even say things that are insensitive or stupid. That happened to me back when I was going through chemo."

"I'm sure I was one of the ones who said stupid things. Gosh, I hope you've forgiven me."

"No, you didn't. Don't worry about what you said. It was a long time ago, and thank God, I've been okay since."

"Thank God," I said. I tried to remember what I had said to her back then, as we were becoming friends and she was in shock about her diagnosis. I hadn't known anyone with cancer before. I hadn't known what to say, and anything I did say felt awkward. She had gotten through her treatment, and our friendship had grown over time. Ever since, I'd never considered the possibility that I or anyone in my family would get cancer. I hadn't worried that Annette's skin issue could be cancerous, and I'd never even stressed out about mammograms.

Susan explained Emily's situation and told me about what their family had gone through after she was diagnosed. As I'd thought, the doctors had watched her tumor for several years. It didn't grow in size and didn't cause Emily any problems. Eventually, they said there was no need to keep on watching it, and now she was doing fine.

"Julie," said Susan, "anytime you need to talk, you just call me. Night or day. I'm so sorry you're going through this, girl. Just remember, I'm here for you, okay?"

"Thanks so much," I said, grateful for her and for our friendship.

* * *

On Friday afternoon, the shutter man showed up and installed the plantation shutters I had ordered for the new bedroom window. I checked that item off my list. The only thing left was to get our den furniture recovered. I'd picked a chocolate brown plush fabric for the sofa, and several pillows in lighter accent colors; two chairs would be redone in a neutral tone. The project had been a joy to plan and to get underway in the spring, and I was thankful that we had the funds to do it. But now that our world had changed, it felt more like a minor problem that I had to get wrapped up.

That evening, a half hour after Dennis got home from work, Jack joined us in the den where we were sitting, having a drink. He wore a big smile.

"Houston, we have landed," he said. "I feel *much* better."

"Wonderful," I said, smiling.

Dennis flashed a smile at me and then at Jack. "It's the simple things."

Jack laughed. "Can we go out to eat at Dave & Buster's tomorrow night, Dad?"

"Sure, but do you think you'll feel up to it? You won't be too tired?"

"Yeah, I think so. Let's try it, anyway."

"Okay," said Dennis. "We could get there kind of early, and see how you feel. That all right?"

"Yeah." Jack sat down on the sofa and let out a sigh. "I'll be glad to get these staples out next week."

"What time is the appointment on Tuesday?" Dennis asked me.

"Eleven-fifteen."

"I'm going to work at home that morning so I can go with you and Mom. Okay, Jack?"

"Great. Thanks, Dad."

"No problem. You and I are going to the Braves game that night too, remember? If you feel like it."

"Oh, yeah, Dad. That'll be fun."

"Wanna watch *Lost* together after dinner?" I asked the two of them. We had been renting episodes of the show through Netflix and watching them as a family.

"Sure," said Jack.

It seemed strange to be doing things like watching movies and planning nights out. On the other hand, it gave me a feeling of order in the midst of our chaos. Like if we kept living our lives as if Jack weren't "sick," then I could temporarily forget that he was. I was all for doing anything to escape the reality of our situation, or at least to ignore it, for the time being.

After Jack got ready for bed that night, I went into his room and sat down on the edge of his bed. For the first ten minutes, we talked about the *Lost* episode, and then he turned to me and sighed. "Mom, I miss my friends from college."

"Well, you're probably not alone there. Everyone has gone home, or somewhere, for the summer."

"I know, but...." His eyes began to fill with tears.

"I'm sorry, honey—"

"It's just that—I knew I wouldn't see most of my friends this summer, but I thought I'd get to see *some* people, and now I've gotta get well, and—"

"I know."

"—and, I can't help it, I've been on Facebook, and I've read a bunch of updates about all the fun things people are doing, and it makes me feel so—*lonely*." He wiped his eyes. "Mom, I just feel left out. Kind of forgotten."

My heart sank with the knowledge that he was so sad, and worse, that there was nothing I could do about it. Damn Facebook. It had been invented to help kids feel socially connected, but right now, it was doing the opposite for Jack—something he definitely didn't need on top of everything else.

I reached for his hand and squeezed it. "Have you told any of your friends what's going on?"

He shook his head. "No one except Matt, Jason and Brendan. I talked to them on the phone."

"Do you feel like telling more people?"

"No. I don't want to talk about it, because I don't even want to think about it. They understand."

"Good."

"I just feel like, if I did talk about it, people would feel awkward or weird around me, you know?"

"Yeah, I know. People might not know what to say. I'm glad you have Jason, Matt and Brendan."

"Me, too."

"As for Facebook, I don't know what to–"

"It's all right," he said, recovering. "I mean, I don't want what's happening to me to be out on Facebook. Now that I told you this, I feel a little better. I can't start feeling sorry for myself. If I do, I'll feel even worse."

"I think you're doing a great job handling everything."

"Thanks, Mom. Goodnight."

I gave him a hug. "Goodnight, honey." I left the room and closed his door, feeling overwhelmed with despair.

* * *

The next morning, as I had planned to do for months, I went to the annual Atlanta Writers Conference at a hotel near the airport to pitch my first novel to a literary agent. Right after my fifteen-minute session that afternoon, I left the hotel to drive home. The last thing I cared about was whether the agent would request to read my manuscript, but I was glad to have met him and attended the conference, if for no other reason than to distract myself for a few hours. When I arrived home around three o'clock, Jack was taking a nap, and Dennis was puttering around the house.

"We're on for tonight," he said. "Let's leave around six, okay?"

"Sure." The closest Dave & Buster's was in Gwinnett County, about a thirty-minute drive from our house.

When we arrived in the parking lot, Jack needed Brian's arm to lean on to walk from the car to the restaurant's entrance.

"You sure this is a good idea?" Dennis asked Jack. "We could always reschedule."

"No, Dad, I really want to try it. I'm hungry, too."

"Okay. It's just that you seem really beat." Dennis and I exchanged worried glances. "But we're here. Let's get a table and order right away."

"Sounds good," said Jack. "Then we can play pool or whatever."

But that wasn't to be. Before our dinner was served, Jack was hardly able to keep his eyes open. He ate what he could, and then we paid the check.

"I'm sorry, Dad," he said as we traipsed out of the restaurant. "Thanks for trying."

Dennis gave him a tender look. "Don't worry about it. You made a valiant effort." He put his arm around Jack and walked with him to the car. We were home before eight o'clock, and Jack went straight to bed.

* * *

On Tuesday, the three of us drove to Dr. Tomaras' office, next to the hospital. Jack signed in at the counter, and a nurse called us in to an examination room. A Physician's Assistant entered and said he would remove the staples, and the doctor would be in afterward.

"This shouldn't hurt," the P. A. said to Jack.

Jack braced himself for discomfort and didn't flinch while the P. A. used a metal instrument resembling a large jackhammer on his head and abdomen. I held my breath as I watched, hoping it really was painless.

When he was done, Jack spoke quietly. "Actually, dude, it *did* hurt."

"I'm sorry," said the P. A. "But they're out now, and everything looks good. No signs of infection. I'll let Dr. Tomaras know you're ready to see him."

Shortly after, the doctor walked in, shook our hands and then washed his. "You're looking good, Jack. How do you feel?"

"Fine—a lot better. But tired. When can I drive?"

"I'm not exactly sure—it depends on when you feel up to it. When you do, start with short distances and familiar routes."

"Okay. I have a volunteer job this Saturday night in Midtown—"

The doctor held up a hand. "First, see how you do with driving this week, okay?"

"I can take him and pick him up on Saturday night if I have to," I said.

"That could work," said the doctor.

"I've also got an internship job in Decatur, starting Monday."

"It's only four hours a day, in the mornings," I added. "Can he do it?"

"Again, if you're feeling up to it," said Dr. Tomaras. "What kind of job is it?"

"It's a drama camp for high school kids called Atlanta Street Theatre. It's in a church. Me and five other college students will be helping run it."

"That sounds like fun. I don't see why you can't. Remember, though, full recovery from the surgery you had is five weeks, so the fatigue you feel right now is normal. Just take it easy over the next couple of weeks."

"Okay," said Jack.

"Now, I've ordered a post-op MRI of the brain for Monday. I believe it's scheduled for three o'clock. After we're done here, I'm sending you over to Northside Imaging Center for three MRIs on your spine: thoracic, cervical, and lumbar."

"*Three?*" asked Jack. "How long will that take?"

"A while–about forty-five minutes or so for each. I'll write you a prescription for a sedative, if you think you'll need it. The nurse will tell you where to go–it's right down the street, not over at the hospital."

"Why do I have to have this?"

"We need to be sure there are no spinal tumors. It's something we check for anytime there's a brain tumor."

Jack threw me a look of alarm.

"It's okay," said Dennis, placing his hand on Jack's arm. "We're going with you. Don't worry."

"Yes, don't worry," said the doctor. "This is just to make sure. I'll call you with the results tomorrow, and I want to see you again on Thursday. You can make your appointment on your way out."

We picked up the sedative at a pharmacy in the building and then drove down the street. The imaging center was located on the ground floor of the same building as Omni Eye Services. We entered and checked in, then sat down together in the small waiting room.

In a few minutes, two technicians came to get Jack, and said he'd be finished in about three hours.

He stood and lumbered toward them.

"You can listen to the radio if you want to, Jack," said one of the techs. "What kind of music do you like?"

"Hip-hop."

"Okay." She smiled and led him through a door.

Dennis and I exchanged glances. He pulled out his phone, checked his messages, and reached for my hand. "Jule, I'm going to step out into the lobby to make a few calls."

"Okay." I watched him walk out the glass door and put the phone to his ear. I fetched my Kindle from my purse and pulled up the book I was reading to distract myself from what was happening to my son. My eyes passed over the words, and every minute or less, I clicked to turn the page, but I couldn't concentrate.

It was after four o'clock when we arrived back home, and even though Jack had spent most of the afternoon lying on a table, he was exhausted. He and Dennis decided to bag the Braves game, and after dinner, we watched another episode of *Lost*.

* * *

QUICK NOTE   **May 18, 2010**

I removed Mr. McDermott's staples in the office today without difficulty. His incision is C/D/I with no signs of infection. His shunt depresses and refills well.

I gave him an RX for Valium to help with his MRIs he has scheduled for today. He is getting an MRI of the C/T/L spines.

Chapter 4

May 19 - May 29

Life's under no obligation to give us what we expect.

— Margaret Mitchell

On Wednesday afternoon, I was about to start the car to drive home from the grocery store when my cell phone buzzed. It was Dr. Tomaras.

"Mrs. McDermott, great news. Jack's spine is clear."

"Oh, thank God."

The doctor's news, though welcome, was like the dissipation of a fast-approaching tornado that I'd been powerless to spot. I hadn't even let myself think about the prospect of spinal tumors, but now it hit me that they certainly had been possible. But before I'd even begun to worry, I didn't have to. My capacity for worry was already completely filled by the brain tumor.

I stared out the windshield, breathed in and exhaled. My eyes rested on a line of tall trees that served as a natural fence between the parking lot and the road–trees that I had driven past for years. The outside world was the same, but my world–Jack's world–was in serious danger, even with this good news.

"Hello? Mrs. McDermott? Are you there?"

"What? Yes, I'm here. I'm sorry, Doctor–what were you saying?"

"That's okay. I was just saying that I'll see you all in my office tomorrow at two o'clock."

"Yes, see you then."

"We can talk about the next steps. Remember, Jack's post-op MRI is scheduled for Monday afternoon."

"I remember. Thank you so much. See you tomorrow."

I called Dennis to tell him the news.

"Thank God!" he said. "I hadn't even considered the idea of spinal tumors, though."

"Me, neither. But what a relief."

"I'll come home at lunch tomorrow so I can go to the appointment with you and Jack."

"Good. See you tonight."

When Dennis walked in the door that evening around six, Jack was in the basement playing video games with Brian. Though they weren't especially close, I felt comforted that Brian was home, and that he hung out with Jack sometimes. Annette was going to her track banquet this evening, but we weren't going; she'd gotten a ride with a teammate who lived in the neighborhood. She'd healed well from her surgery, and her follow-up appointment was the end of next week.

More than ever, I was thankful that Annette was who she was: self-reliant, savvy and tough. She'd always been that way, even as a child, and was adept at controlling her emotions. She had done a great job recovering from her surgery, and balancing school and sports activities in recent days. She was doing all she could to avoid putting more strain on me, and she seemed to know I was grateful. She was worried about Jack, and probably scared, but she was pushing through and handling things on her own. She hadn't wanted to talk about what was happening, and I suspected it was because she didn't want to risk getting emotional. But that was fine—it was the way she coped, and it was working.

Dennis went up to get changed, and Kathy O'Barr called me, asking if we wanted her and Tom to come over to talk about Jack.

"They can be here in half an hour," I told Dennis. "We can eat dinner after." The two of us sat down in the den to talk until the O'Barrs arrived.

When the doorbell rang, we went to answer it together, greeted our friends, and ushered them in.

Tom began the discussion. "You guys may already know this, but Dr. Tomaras usually refers his patients to M.D. Anderson. He'll probably do so at your appointment tomorrow. However, Kathy and I think you should talk to some other physicians around the country as well."

"Like who?" said Dennis.

"Well, Emory's a possibility," said Kathy. "UCSF is also a really good place."

"UCSF?" I asked.

"The University of California at San Francisco. They're known for treating brain tumors. You could make an appointment out there, and one in Houston."

My eyes widened. "You mean, travel to California and to Texas, just to talk to them?" Of course, we'd do that if we had to, but it sounded very complicated, and stressful.

Tom looked from me to Dennis. "You may be able to send them copies of the disk, ask them to take a look at it, and see if they'll call you to discuss it first. Don't you think so, Kathy?"

"It's certainly worth asking. Some of the doctors may be open to an initial phone conference. If you let us have Jack's post-op MRI disk, we'll get some copies made. We could contact them and send the disks out on your behalf."

"Thank you," said Dennis.

"Wait," said Tom. "Two other hospitals we think you should consider are Johns Hopkins and Duke. Both are very, very good."

"You'll contact them, too?" I asked.

"Certainly," said Tom. "Why don't we make six copies of the disk?"

"That would be great," said Dennis.

"Good," said Kathy. "Here's another thing we could do, if you want us to. There's a doctor right here in our neighborhood who's a radiologist at Emory. Her name is Pat Hudgins. She lives right down the street from you. Her job is to read and evaluate MRIs. She's also a neurology professor at Emory University. We've known her for a number of years—she's really, really good."

Tom spoke up. "We could get in touch with Pat and see if she'd be willing to take a look at the MRI. We could give her a copy of the disk, and the four of us could meet with her at her house and she can tell us what she thinks."

Dennis looked at me, raised his eyebrows and gave a slight nod.

"That would be great," I said. "If you think she'd do it."

Kathy nodded. "I think she will. I'll call her and let you know. She'll give us her honest opinion, and tell us whether Emory's the right place."

"It *would* be really convenient if we could go someplace here in Atlanta," said Dennis. "No matter what she advises though, thanks for approaching her for us."

I let out a small sigh. This thing was really happening—our boy would be seeing oncologists and neurosurgeons very soon. I was still clinging to the hope that the tumor was benign, but that hope was weakening with every passing hour. I turned to Tom. "I haven't said anything to Jack about the idea of going to a doctor somewhere out of town."

"Don't—not yet," said Tom. "Dr. Tomaras will, though. Go to your appointment tomorrow, get the MRI done, and then give us the disk so we can make the copies. Then we'll go from there. We're in this thing with you guys, okay?"

"Thanks so much," I said.

"No problem," said Kathy. "Hang in there."

* * *

The following afternoon, Jack, Dennis and I walked into an exam room at Dr. Tomaras' office and waited. The doctor entered the room a few minutes later and shook Jack's hand.

"It's wonderful news that your tumor hasn't spread to the spine," he said. He gave Jack a quick eye exam and had him perform some gross motor movements. "Any headaches?"

"No."

"How about reading? Is that better?"

"Yeah, a *lot* better."

"Good!" Turning to me, he asked, "Have you scheduled a follow up appointment with the ophthalmologist?"

"No—I didn't know he needed one."

"He does. I'd like him to see the same doctor he saw the day you came in to the hospital. Try to get an appointment this week or next."

"Okay," I said.

"Now, let's talk about the brain tumor," said the doctor, looking at Jack.

"Will he have radiation therapy?" I asked.

Dr. Tomaras looked at me, then at Dennis. "Well, before any treatment, Jack needs a biopsy to identify the tumor. The problem is that, with it so deep in his brain, the procedure is not without risk."

Dennis crossed his arms in front of his chest and studied the doctor's face. I guessed what he was about to say; he'd told me earlier that if at all possible, he didn't want anyone cutting into Jack's head and "messing around in there."

"But if he's going to have radiation, no matter what type of tumor it is, then why have the biopsy?" asked Dennis. "I mean, why do a risky procedure, if you know the treatment will be radiation, in any case?"

The doctor shook his head. "The treatment depends on the type of tumor. We won't know that, until we get results from a biopsy. It's not clear that it will be radiation. And I don't know of any oncologist who would treat him without first seeing the biopsy results."

"What exactly happens in a biopsy?" asked Jack.

The doctor faced him. "The surgeon goes in and removes a tiny piece of tissue from your tumor and sends it over to pathology. Then the pathologists identify the tumor."

"And then?" said Jack.

"Then a treatment plan is developed. That might include radiation therapy, but at this point, we don't know."

"What about gamma knife?" I asked. "I've heard that's sometimes done for brain tumors." Susan had mentioned it when we talked.

Jack grabbed the arms of the chair. "What's gamma knife?"

"Don't worry, it's not a knife like what you might be thinking," said the doctor. "It's a specific kind of targeted radiation that's very precise. Unfortunately, I don't think it's going to be appropriate here, because of the tumor's location. Again, we have to have a diagnosis. I'll refer you to my contacts at M.D. Anderson in Houston, and to those at some other hospitals, if you wish."

"Okay," said Jack, a look of bewilderment on his face. The necessity of traveling to see other doctors was apparently sinking in.

"Thank you, Doctor," said Dennis. "We've been in touch with our internist too, and he said we may want to approach Emory, UCSF, Johns Hopkins, and Duke."

The doctor paused for a second. "Yes, those are all good places, all with very good reputations. I can give you a referral to some contacts in San Francisco. You can get in touch with Emory if you wish, and Johns Hopkins is very good, too." He hesitated for a second, and then cocked his head. "I'm not too sure about Duke, though. They're known to have kind of a cowboy mentality."

My eyebrows shot up. "What do you mean, 'cowboy mentality'?"

"Oh, don't get me wrong. Duke is very, very good, and they have some great neurosurgeons. I just meant that they seem to have a shoot-first approach sometimes."

I swallowed and fought against my feelings of panic. We were swimming in a sea of peril, with life preservers only barely visible on the horizon. What was going to happen to my boy? I glanced at Jack, wondering if he felt the same.

"Now, go ahead and get the eye exam. My secretary will be in touch with the referral information."

"Thank you, Doctor," said Dennis.

"You're welcome. Good luck. Let me know if I can help you in any way."

* * *

PEACHTREE NEUROSURGERY   **May 20, 2010**

Mr. McDermott returns with his family for further discussion of his pineal region mass and his shunt. We have discussed the options of empiric radiation therapy versus seeking additional opinions, which I have encouraged them to do. We have given them the names of physicians at M.D. Anderson and UCSF, and also encouraged them to contact local physicians at Emory. We will obtain a post op MRI study, and he will follow up with the ophthalmologist who saw him preoperatively. His blurred vision is much better, and his headaches have completely resolved.

- Christopher R. Tomaras, M.D.

* * *

On Friday morning, Jack wanted to time the route for his internship job starting on Monday. We decided that I would follow him in my car, just in case.

Less than two miles from our house, he pulled into a Kroger parking lot and rolled down his window. I pulled next to him. He said he was having trouble seeing the yellow line in the road and didn't feel he could make it to Decatur. We went back home and agreed to go in my car. The round trip took us about an hour. When we got home again, he insisted he could do it on Monday, but we agreed that I would follow him.

On Saturday evening, he was scheduled to go to Whole World Theatre in Midtown for his first night as a volunteer, but neither of us thought he should make the drive home after dark. I took him down there, planning to either go to the show, or go home and come back and pick him up. As we walked the fifty yards from the parking lot to the entrance, he seemed unsteady. I put my arm around him.

"Gosh, Mom, I'm so tired," he said. "It's been two weeks since the surgery. I'm *sick* of being so tired all the time. And now that we're here, I don't know if I can do this. Actually, I *know* I can't. I don't know what to say to the manager."

I could help him here; this was the kind of problem that my mom-years had trained me to solve. "Okay, look. We'll go in and find him. Then you can explain what's going on, or I will, if you want."

"No, I'll talk to him. But I feel so bad about it. I was supposed to start last week, and when I called then and explained about the surgery, he was really understanding. When I talked to him yesterday, I was *sure* I'd be fine tonight."

"He'll be understanding again. Don't worry."

We climbed the few wooden steps to the theatre door and entered the small lobby. The room was filled with people, most of them under forty. Some stood in small groups holding drinks, and some sat on brightly colored sofas and chairs. Others crowded at the bar, over to our right. The walls were covered with posters featuring theatre cast members.

Jack stopped in front of a black podium just inside the entrance and asked the receptionist for the manager. In a few seconds, a thirty-something man appeared. I stayed silent while Jack started to explain and apologize. The manager looked up at his unsteady eyes, then at his shaved, scarred head, and insisted that he go home and call back when he felt better.

When we got home, Jack went straight to bed. I told Dennis what had happened, and we sat down to have a drink.

Later that night, I was grateful that Jack was already asleep when I went up to go to bed.

* * *

On Monday morning, Jack woke up around seven-thirty. We sat together in the den for a few minutes, watching TV and drinking coffee while Dennis got ready for work.

"Would you make me an omelet, Mom?"

I smiled. Jack and his siblings had known before they could talk that their father was the family cook, but they were aware of the dishes I could prepare. Omelets were one of the few. "Sure. American cheese?"

"That would be great. And toast?"

"No problem." I walked into the kitchen to make one of Jack's favorite meals—the same one I would fix for him every weekday morning for the next five weeks.

At a few minutes after eight, he was dressed and ready to go. Knowing traffic would be heavy, he had decided to leave by eight-fifteen to be sure to arrive on time.

As agreed, I followed him in my car. He did fine on the drive down, and pulled into the parking lot at about ten minutes before nine. I parked, walked over to him and gave him a hug. I looked up at his eyes. "If you need me, just call, okay?"

"Okay." He smiled. "I'll be fine."

"Okay. Good luck."

"Thanks, Mom. I love you."

"Love you, too."

Back at home, I got busy with housework and chores, keeping my phone with me at all times. When I was done, I sat down at my computer to work on my novel.

Shortly after one p.m., Jack called and said he was going to stop at Chick-fil-A on the way home. I was glad he let me know, and that he sounded happy about how his first day had gone. When he got back, he wanted to chill out and watch TV for an hour or so until it was time for the post-op MRI.

* * *

NORTHSIDE - RADIOLOGY

Date of Specimen: 05/24/2010 14:58

Physician: Tomaras, Christopher

MRPD BRAIN WO/W CONTRAST

Comparison is made with previous study from 5/8/10.

FINDINGS: In the interim, the patient has undergone placement of a ventricular catheter which extends to the region of the frontal horn of the right lateral ventricle. Complex solid and cystic mass is again noted to involve the pineal gland region. Overall, the mass appears slightly larger on the current study. It measures approximately 3.3 cm in greatest AP dimension as compared to approximately 3.0 by my measurement at the same level on the previous study. In transverse dimension, it measures up to approximately 2.8 cm as compared to 2.5 cm on the previous study. In craniocaudal dimension, it measures up to approximately 2.8 cm as compared to 2.5 cm on the previous study.

IMPRESSION: Since the previous study of 5/8/10, there has been mild interval enlargement of pineal region complex cystic and solid mass. The cystic components of the mass appear to have slightly increased in size.

* * *

NOTE   5-25-10

Telicia called from M.D. Anderson and said that she spoke with the mom and she said they do not want to go to M.D. Anderson but they want a phone conference with the doctors there.

That is between them. I am not sure if that is even an option?

I left a message with MD Tues.

I agree that is not usually how it is done. I have given them names of other places and they had their own contacts that they wanted to explore.

- Chris R. Tomaras, M.D.

* * *

On Wednesday, Jack came home from his internship job to find me at work on the computer. The hours I spent writing fiction were my therapy and escape, and I was glad I'd started writing this novel before our world had caved in.

"Hey, Mom, I talked to my friend Matt. He invited me to come spend the weekend at his family's lake house."

Alarm bells rang in my head. I trusted the boys, but I didn't want to be away from Jack anytime that he wasn't at work. The lake was a lot farther away, and I was still afraid that he might have a seizure. "Are his parents going to be there?"

He rolled his eyes. "Yeah, Mom. Don't worry!"

"I'm just asking. When does he want you to come up?"

"Saturday morning. I'll come home on Sunday night, since I have to work on Monday."

"Are you sure you feel like going?"

"Yeah. If I get tired, I'll find somewhere to lay down and take a nap." He was reassuring himself as well as me, I thought.

"What would you do up there? Just hang out, go out in a boat, or what?" Jack had never water-skied; he wasn't a lake person, and we weren't a lake family.

"Just hang out with Matt. Maybe go tubing or swimming."

"What about driving all the way up there? Do you think you can do it?" Lake Lanier was over an hour north of us, up Highway 400. Although Jack had done okay this week on surface streets, he hadn't yet tackled the expressway.

"I don't know. I hadn't thought about that. Maybe."

"I could take you up there, and come get you when you're ready to come home."

He raised his eyebrows. "You'd do that?"

"Sure. But first I want to call Dr. Tomaras' office and make sure he says it's all right for you to go."

"Mom—"

"Just let me call, okay?"

"All right," he said, a look of resignation on his face. He didn't want me "momming" him (our family's word for helicoptering), but at the same time, he seemed to understand my concern, and appreciate it.

That evening, he proposed a second plan. The Braves were playing the Pittsburgh Pirates on Friday night, and he wanted to invite Jason to come down from Athens to go to the game. They could take MARTA to Underground Atlanta and then take the bus to Turner Field.

"Jason's never been to a Braves game," Jack said to me and Dennis. "I think he's really gonna like it."

I was apprehensive again, and had a real fear that something would happen to him while he was gone. However, after our talk when he'd told me about how lonely he felt, I empathized with his wish to see his buddies. He'd been through a lot so far, and he was dealing with things the best he could.

"That sounds like fun," said Dennis, unconcerned about the outing. "Will he want to stay overnight? Tell him he can if he wants to."

"Okay. Knowing Jason, though, he'll probably wanna head back after the game."

"Whatever," I said, glad that his friends wanted to see him. "Just be careful, okay?"

"We'll be fine, Mom."

* * *

TELEPHONE NOTE   **May 27, 2010**
His mother called yesterday to say that he is doing well and ask if he can go to Lake Lanier Saturday to Monday with some friends. No skiing or anything like that, but can he swim?

MD ANDERSON RETURN CALL   **May 27, 2010**
MD Anderson returned your call regarding Mr. McDermott.

* * *

Jack's follow-up visit with the ophthalmologist was the next day at four-fifteen. We arrived shortly after four and sat down in the large waiting room filled with patients, most of whom were much closer to my age than his.

After a few minutes, Dr. Sturdy strode into the room from behind the receptionist's counter. Smiling broadly, he walked right over to Jack. We stood up, and he shook Jack's hand and greeted us warmly. The other patients looked up from their magazines and watched, a bit awestruck. No mere nurse had fetched my son, but eventually, one would come for them.

Back in an exam room, Jack brought the eye doctor up to date.

"Wow. I'm so sorry you're dealing with this," Dr. Sturdy said, his face full of compassion. "Your eyes look much better now—I can already tell."

"Good. I can see a *whole* lot better now."

"That's great! Ready to get started with the exam?"

Jack nodded, a resigned but cheerful look on his face. "Just tell me what to do."

The doctor put him through the same set of exams he had before: simple vision tests and the peripheral vision exercise. Then he took new photos of Jack's retinas and optic discs and showed us the color printouts. They looked similar to the previous ones, but he said they showed a marked improvement.

"Really?" said Jack. "But there's still a lot of red."

"There will be, for a while. The good news is, it's getting better. The surgery took a *lot* of pressure off your eyes."

"Thank you, Doctor," I said. Thoughts of what would have happened to Jack's sight if the surgery hadn't been done that night ran through my head. I shuddered.

"Good luck," said Dr. Sturdy, looking at me and Jack. He handed me the paperwork for today's visit. "Let me know how things go with you, okay, Jack?"

"Will do," said the patient.

We drove the short distance home talking about the doctor.

"I really like him," said Jack.

"Me, too. He's young, but he's good, and he explains everything."

"Yeah, he does. He treats me well, too."

"That's really important. He seems happy to be an eye doctor–and to be able to help people."

That evening, as we had planned, Kathy and Tom came to pick up Dennis and me to go to Cocktails in the Garden, held on Thursday evenings at the Atlanta Botanical Gardens. The kids were on their own for dinner. During the fifteen minute drive to Midtown, the four of us talked about our children and carefully avoided the topic of Jack's tumor. After we entered the Gardens and bought our drinks, we paired up and strolled down the path. Dennis and Tom walked slightly ahead of Kathy and me.

"So, how are you doing?" she asked.

"Okay, I guess. I think I'm still in shock, frankly."

"I completely understand. I would be, too. Anytime you want to talk, just call me, okay? *If* you want to talk."

I nodded. We continued chatting, but my ear was pricked by bits of conversation I overheard our husbands having. Dennis hadn't given up on avoiding a biopsy, and I listened to him questioning our internist and friend about it.

"Well," said Tom, "I don't know if that's possible—"

"Why, though?" asked Dennis. "I mean, it seems like the treatment would be the same—"

"I don't know about that," said Tom, shaking his head. "Like Tomaras told you…"

Their pace quickened just enough to take them out of earshot, and his words faded, but didn't coax me to draw closer. If Tom wasn't offering better news, I didn't want to listen.

Kathy and I continued walking behind the men and chatted, stopping here and there. "So, Julie. I imagine by now you've gone on *webmd*—right?" She gave me a measured look.

I nodded. "I did the other day, but I didn't get very far. It was too scary. I feel like I should wait until we know more."

"Good. I think you're smart to wait. I mean, I can't tell you not to go online, but as your friend, I wouldn't advise doing it yet. If you go on *webmd* and the other medical sites right now and read about all the different kinds of brain tumors, it'll scare you to death. I think you'd be wiser to wait until you find out what type of tumor Jack has. Even then, I would try to stay away from the Internet, and just listen to the doctors."

"Yeah, you're probably right."

"I mean, don't get me wrong. You guys should want to educate yourselves, and I know you do. But there's so much out there online that doesn't—or won't—apply to Jack. I wouldn't spend my time reading about all the bad kinds of tumors. I would just talk directly with the doctors about Jack's particular situation. You're going to have that opportunity soon enough."

"Oh, Kathy. I can't believe this is happening."

"I know. I'm so sorry." She put her arm around me. "Hang in there. Just focus on the next step in the process."

* * *

That night, Jack asked me to come talk to him in his room again before he went to sleep.

"How's the internship going?"

"I really like it. It's a lot of fun, but it's lot of work, too. And there's a lot of drama going on between some of the people there. No pun intended."

I smiled. "I'm glad you'd already found this job in April."

"Yeah. It really helps that I have something to do every day, so I don't have to think about *this*." He pointed to his head and raised his eyebrows.

"Have you told anybody there about it? Like, about your scar, or why your hair is so short?"

"I told them I had surgery, but not a whole lot else."

"You know, we *could* tell the people in our church what's going on if you want. They might want to pray for you."

But should we do that, before we even told my family? My parents went to a different church, so they wouldn't know if we did. But I wouldn't feel right about it.

"No, Mom. I don't want to. When they pray for the sick at mass, I don't want my name called. I don't want people to hear it and look at me and think, 'there's the guy with the brain tumor.' I just don't want *anyone* to feel sorry for me." He wiped one eye.

I took a deep breath, and then let it out. Once the word was out to everyone, including my parents, it would have comforted me to have his name called during the prayer petitions at mass.

But Jack's feelings were more important than mine. The last few Sundays, at his request, we had sat in a side area, entering through the back door at the last second, and exiting the moment mass was over. "Okay, fine. We won't ask for your name to be called. We won't even tell the pastor what's going on, unless you want to. During mass, after they go through the names, and then say that general prayer for all the sick of our parish, *that* can be when people at church pray for you."

"Good."

"Do you feel ready to tell Grandma and Granddad now?"

"No–not yet. I want to wait until we know what my treatment's gonna be, and where we have to go for it."

The longer we waited, the tougher it would be. But maybe he had a point about knowing what was ahead of us first. "Okay, honey. I understand."

He grabbed my hand. "I'm gonna *make* it, right, Mom?"

"Of *course* you're gonna make it! We've just gotta get through this, and then you'll be fine. I meant it when I said we're not taking 'no' for an answer."

He sighed. "That's what I think, too, Mom. It's not gonna be 'no,' it's gonna be 'yes.' Yes, I *can.* Yes, I *will.*"

"Whatever we have to do, okay?" I blinked, holding back tears. My throat was tight.

"Okay. I love you, Mom."

"I love you, too." I squeezed his hand and kissed his forehead. "Goodnight, Jack."

I climbed into bed a few minutes later and snuggled up to my husband, who held me close.

"How is he?"

I sighed. "He's hanging in there."

"How about you?"

"Oh, Dennis. I don't know. I keep telling him he's gonna make it, but–I'm scared."

He pulled me closer. "Me, too, babe. But I'm so glad he wants to talk to you at night."

"I am, too."

"You be there for him, and I'll be here for you. Okay?" His voice had broken. "You be his rock, and I'll be *your* rock."

"Okay," I said, letting the tears flow.

Then I cried myself to sleep.

* * *

On Friday evening, Jason arrived at our house. Jack ushered him into the kitchen and introduced him to me and Dennis. Smiling, Jason greeted us and shook our hands. Two years older than Jack and at least four inches shorter, he'd served as the leader of the college improv group that Jack had joined. After a few minutes of small talk, the two of them left to go to the game.

I knew they'd be fine getting there and back; Jack had gone to many Braves games and knew his way around. But—maybe because he'd be in the midst of a crowd, at night—the possibility that something could happen to him while he was gone never left my thoughts. I kept my cell phone next to me that evening, and put it on my nightstand when I went to bed.

When Jack got up the next morning, he said that Jason had driven back to Athens after the game. Then he told Dennis and me all about their evening.

They had taken MARTA to Underground Atlanta and bought milkshakes at Johnny Rockets. Then they walked around, joining throngs of Braves fans who filled the touristy downtown mall. As they made their way over to the bus for Turner Field, three guys wearing identical Jason Heyward jerseys strode side by side a few feet ahead of them. Jason had pointed at them and quipped, "Hey Jack—how many jerseys do you see? Are you seeing triple?"

They had broken out laughing at the inside joke. Jack laughed now as he told the story and Dennis and I giggled.

"That Jason," said Dennis. "I think I like him."

"Yeah," said Jack. "He's a great guy."

Later that morning, I drove Jack to Matt Ryan's house on Lake Lanier. Because the evening at the Braves game had gone well, I felt somewhat reassured that the lake trip would, too. We pulled into the driveway and Matt bounded out to greet us. "Hey, Jack! How are you, man?"

"Doing okay," said Jack, unfolding himself from the car and giving Matt a man-hug. "Great to see you!"

"Hello there, Mrs. McDermott. Welcome to the lake!"

"Thanks, Matt. I'll just go in and say hi to your mom, if that's okay."

"Sure, she's in the kitchen. Come on."

We followed Matt into the house where he introduced me to his mother, Liz. After the guys disappeared, she and I chatted for a few minutes and exchanged cell phone numbers.

"Now, don't worry about him," she said as I was about to head home. "We'll take good care of him, I promise."

"Thanks. The doctor said he's fine to go swimming, but it's probably not a good idea to do much else."

"No water skiing and no jet skiing," she said. "How about tubing? It's easy, and he can't get hurt."

"I don't know. I think it's okay. I'll let Jack decide."

"I'm sure he'll have fun, no matter what they do."

"Thanks, Liz. I'll come get him tomorrow evening."

I drove home and spent the next few hours writing and catching up on household chores and trying not to worry. Late that afternoon, Jack called.

He had gone out on the lake with Matt and had gone tubing on his stomach. When he had hit the wake, the part of the shunt in his abdomen had caused him discomfort and pain, and now he wanted to come home. He had told Matt that he wished he could stay, but he was worried he might feel worse later tonight.

"I'll come get you right now," I said.

"Thanks, Mom. I'm sorry about this." I could hear disappointment and relief in his voice.

"No problem, honey."

"Mr. Ryan said he and Matt can take me to meet you at a shopping center off of 400, right next to the exit we took. They'll wait there with me—we'll be in a black pickup truck. Can you meet us in about an hour?"

"Sure."

I jumped in the car and headed north. Two trips to the lake and back in one day was a lot, but considering how Jack felt, I was glad he had decided to come home. Around six o'clock, I pulled into the parking lot and looked for the truck. When I parked next to it, Matt and Jack got out and Matt's father walked over to meet me.

"He seems to be doing okay now, but earlier he didn't feel so well," he said. "I think he was right to call you, though." He paused and looked into my eyes. "Mrs. McDermott, I'm so sorry about Jack."

I stopped for a second. "Did he tell you everything?"

He said in a low voice, "He did. We're all hoping and praying for the best. I know he's got a rough road ahead."

Jack ambled around to the passenger side of my car. He turned to his friend. "Thanks for inviting me, Matt. I'm sorry." His face had fallen, and he looked sad and apologetic.

"No problem, man. Hey, take it easy."

"Thank you for bringing me over here, Mr. Ryan."

"You're welcome, Jack. You take care, okay? We're all pulling for you."

Jack and I got in the car and began the drive home. As I merged onto 400 south, I couldn't get the last expression on Mr. Ryan's face off my mind.

He had looked at Jack as if he would never see him again.

Chapter 5

June 1 - 4

Every man has his secret sorrows which the world knows not; and often times we call a man cold when he is only sad.

– Henry Wadsworth Longfellow

On Tuesday, June 1, Dennis and I drove down the street and parked in Pat's driveway, arriving the same time as Kathy and Tom.

"Thanks for coming with us, you guys," I said.

"Happy to do it," said Kathy. "Are you doing all right, Julie?"

"I guess. Jack doesn't know we're doing this meeting…"

"He doesn't need to know," said Kathy. Dennis looked at her and nodded.

Pat met us at her kitchen door, and Tom introduced her to Dennis and me. She greeted us and looked at us with misty eyes. "I'm so sorry you're going through this," she said.

Dennis glanced at me, and then looked at her. "Thank you, and thank you for meeting with us tonight."

"No problem. It's the least I can do." She ushered us into a spacious home office, where a desktop computer anchored the room and books lined nearby shelves. "Okay. Let me get the disk loaded." She produced the copy Tom had given her and inserted it. A few seconds later, a black and white profile image of a head appeared on the monitor.

"Oh," she said. "I see it. Right here." She pointed to a dark area in the middle of the image. "Let me enlarge this and get some measurements."

We waited for a few seconds.

"Okay," said Pat. "Well, this is interesting. Didn't you say that Tomaras told you that first night that he thought it could be a germinoma?"

"Yes," said Dennis.

"In my opinion, that's possible, but I'm not sure. It could definitely be another, more deadly kind of tumor."

My legs felt like jelly. *No. That couldn't be true.*

"What makes you say that?" asked Dennis.

Pat pulled out a large reference book, opened it and began to describe the characteristics of various other types of brain tumors. Everything sounded like Greek. "I could give you my best guess, but I think Tomaras is right about a biopsy. That's going to *have* to happen before your son can get any kind of treatment. And it's going to be risky, considering where this thing is sitting." She shook her head.

"What do you mean?" I said. "How do they do a biopsy?"

She regarded me for a second. "Well, they take a scope-like instrument and insert it very low, right about here"—she pointed to the image on the monitor—"under the skull. The surgeon carefully guides that instrument to the tumor and removes a tiny piece of it. Then they send it over to pathology for analysis."

"How do they get the instrument to the tumor?" I asked. "I don't really understand."

She tilted her head. "It's not without risk, as I said. Whatever the biopsy results, your son's going to have to have the tumor surgically removed, before receiving any type of therapy."

"Invasive brain surgery?" asked Dennis. "Is there any way to avoid that?"

Pat looked straight at him. "Not if you want him to live."

Tears filled my eyes and my whole body felt weak. This could not be happening. "Are you *sure?*"

Pat turned toward me and looked directly into my eyes. "I know this is very difficult to hear. But—you are just going to have to get over this. Your son needs brain surgery. There's no other way to get his tumor out."

Tom put his hand on his chin. "*Must* he have a biopsy first, then? I mean, considering the risks—"

Pat paused. "You may be right, Tom. The surgeon might choose to skip a biopsy, remove the entire mass, and then have it analyzed."

I trembled. Things were being determined much too fast. "Wait a second. Would you explain how they do invasive brain surgery?"

Pat looked at me as if she were talking to a first-grader. She spoke slowly. "They drill into the back of his skull, cut out a small piece of it, and put that in a bowl. Then, they go in and carefully remove the tumor. When they're finished, they put the piece of the skull back and fasten it in place with titanium screws. The whole thing takes several hours."

I felt as if I were going to faint. I grabbed Dennis' arm and looked over at Kathy.

"It's okay, Julie," she said. "There *are* neurosurgeons who do this, who are very, *very* good at what they do. You guys just need to find the right one. Pat, what do you think about Emory?"

Pat cocked her head. "Truthfully, we don't see these very often. I'm not too sure Houston does, either."

"I'll do some checking into that," said Kathy. "I think you're right, though. I've heard Anderson doesn't see many brain tumors."

Tom spoke up. "I would say approach San Francisco, for sure. Also Duke and Johns Hopkins. Do you agree, Pat?"

"Yes. That's exactly what I would do." She stood looking at me and Dennis, her face matter-of-fact, as if she had just handed us a prescription.

"Okay," said Tom. "Dennis and Julie, we'll contact UCSF, Hopkins, and Duke for you, and see if we can send them a copy of the disk. You keep one to send to Anderson, if you choose to do that. You can get their contact info from Tomaras. We'll help you follow up with everybody on the phone, and you decide who you want to make appointments with."

"Sounds like a good plan. Good luck," said Pat. "Let me know if I can do anything to help." She gave each of us a hug, and we said goodbye. Out in the driveway, the O'Barrs said they would contact the hospitals first thing in the morning.

That night, we ate leftovers for dinner. After my nightly chat with Jack in his room, I went to get ready for bed.

"I didn't like that woman," I said to Dennis. "She was so blunt."

"She was pretty direct," said Dennis. "But she seemed very nice. Not much of a bedside manner, though."

"'You are just going to have to get over this,'" I quoted her. "My God! I don't *want* to get over it. I don't want to do it!"

"Babe, I know. I don't want to do it, either. But it looks like we have to, after all. It looks like we don't have a choice."

"Well, we'll see what the doctors say."

"Whatever happens, at least it sounds like he may not have to have a biopsy first."

"Ugh! The way she described the surgery—what they would do—"

"I know, honey. But that might have been exactly what we needed to hear—so we could start to digest it."

"I don't want to, though!" I collapsed under the covers and started crying. "What are we going to do?"

He pulled me close. "I don't know, Jule. I just don't know."

* * *

On Wednesday evening, Jack said that Jason had invited him to come to Athens on Saturday to hang out and spend the night at his apartment. I didn't want him to go—I was afraid he wouldn't be able to make the drive there and back, and I was still afraid that he might have a seizure. It certainly seemed possible, given what I'd learned the few times I'd read about brain tumors online.

Dennis disagreed with me. "Let him go and see his friends. It's only about an hour's drive. I'm sure he can do it. He'll be careful. He hasn't had any seizures, so there's no reason he should have one now."

"But—"

"Julie. I know you're worried, but it's been almost four weeks since the shunt surgery. Hanging out with his friends could be good for him. It's probably exactly what he needs right now."

Reluctantly, I consented, but I knew I would think about him during all the hours that he was gone.

Over the last twenty-four hours, I'd been trying to push what Pat had said out of my mind, but her words kept coming back. If she was right—and chances were, she was—I *was* going to have to get over it: my son was going to have invasive brain surgery—soon.

Kathy and Tom kept us posted about the disks they were sending out to the doctors. They talked to the physicians in San

Francisco, who said they wouldn't even look at the MRI ahead of a visit. If we wanted a conference, we'd have to make an appointment and travel there. We hadn't heard back yet from Johns Hopkins or Duke. We hadn't contacted M.D. Anderson or Emory yet.

We told Jack that the O'Barrs were sending out the disks to the hospitals, and explained that we hoped they would do phone conferences with us. But we didn't tell him what Pat said. We decided to wait until we heard from all the doctors first, in the remote chance that she turned out to be wrong.

In the meantime, I wanted to talk to Dennis' sister, who was a breast cancer survivor. Cathy was six months older than me and had had a mastectomy in her early thirties; since then, she had been cancer-free. She and her husband Steve lived in North Carolina. We saw them more often than anyone else in Dennis' large family, most members of which lived in Texas and Colorado.

Cathy and I had never been close, but our relationship was friendly. We'd gotten married young, the same year. Afterward, our lives had gone in opposite directions. She'd pursued a successful career and had had twin boys in her late thirties. I'd stopped working outside the home in my mid-twenties and had had my youngest child at thirty-five.

On Thursday afternoon, I walked out to the front porch, dialed Cathy's cell and left a message asking her to call when she had time to talk. Then I sat down in one of the two rocking chairs on our porch.

I leaned back in the chair and closed my eyes. A memory flashed in my mind of the Sunday afternoon just days after Annette's birth, when one of the twins had slammed Jack's finger in the heavy back door to our house. Dennis had grabbed him, held him over the kitchen sink, and rinsed the blood away. With his fingertip dangling, Jack had screamed and cried out, "Mommy! Kiss it and make it better!"

Dennis had wrapped the finger and we raced to the emergency room, where a doctor stitched it up. Weeks later, it was completely healed, and ever since, it had been impossible to tell which fingertip had almost been severed. I wanted Jack to be completely healed again now, but this time, getting well was going to be much more difficult.

This time, he might have to fight for his life.

I pushed the memory away and went back in the den, where Jack was watching television, his laptop open in front of him. I went to get a basket full of clothes from the dryer to fold before taking them upstairs.

I set the basket down and Jack started, then turned to me. "Mom! Look at this!" He pointed to the laptop screen.

"What's the matter?"

"Look what Uncle Ross wrote on my Facebook wall!"

Ross was married to Dennis' youngest sister, Maureen. He was in his forties and was Facebook friends with most of the family's younger generation—Jack's cousins—all of whom were Facebook friends with Jack.

I walked over and looked at the screen. Ross' message said: "Jack, you're in all of our thoughts and prayers as you go through the weeks and months ahead. We hope you have a full and speedy recovery!"

I cringed. At least he hadn't mentioned the words "tumor" or "cancer." But the message was obviously a reference to it, and the last thing Jack needed right now was to have his illness outed on Facebook.

He looked up at me, consternation showing on his face. "I thought Grandma Mary told the adults not to say anything!"

"She did. Uncle Ross probably meant well, but he screwed up."

"Mom, everyone who saw this will know! Everyone's gonna be posting comments or messaging me!"

"Maybe they won't. I'm so sorry, honey."

He sighed, leaned back and closed his eyes. "Maybe he meant well, but it still makes me mad. I'm going to delete it." He opened his eyes. "I don't want to talk about it. I just wanna be well. And I wanna be able to go to Texas for vacation without having to talk about it!"

Dennis' family got together every summer for a week-long reunion and "classic" golf tournament, normally in Texas over the week of the Fourth of July. Usually, almost everyone attended. This year's trip was scheduled for July 3-9, and I had booked our plane tickets a few months ago. However, now it was unlikely we'd be going. I assumed Jack had realized that.

"Let's not worry about going to Texas right now," I said. "Let's just focus on today, and on the next few days, okay?"

Jack gave me a look like I'd just said that mom-ism, *We'll see.* "We're still going, aren't we?"

"Honestly, I don't know. If we can, we will. We just have to see what happens."

"It's just that I've really been looking forward to it."

"I know. But let's not worry about it right now, okay?"

He dropped his eyes and looked back at his laptop. I walked away, content to leave the matter unresolved.

An hour later, when Dennis got home from work, I followed him up to our room and told him about Ross' message and Jack's reaction.

"*Damn* it!" he said. "I told my mother to tell everyone not to let the kids know, but here's Ross going and posting it on Facebook! Why don't these people listen?"

I had predicted Dennis would be upset, but I hadn't realized he'd be this angry. However, I knew he wanted to protect Jack and to respect his wish for privacy as much as I did. "I don't know. I'm sure that Ross had good intentions—"

"I don't care! I'm on Jack's side on this one. He doesn't want it to be public knowledge yet, and *he's* the one going through this. It looks like those damn people could respect that!"

I shook my head slowly. "I know."

"I'm gonna call my mom after dinner. No, I'm gonna call her right now—"

"I'm sure it's not her fault."

"I'm sure it isn't, either. But I'm gonna call her and tell her to call everybody out there tonight, and tell them: Dennis said, he's not asking you, he's *telling* you NOT to tell the kids about Jack! And no Facebook messages! If anyone has a problem with that, they can call me directly!'"

As the oldest of his siblings, Dennis was used to giving orders when necessary, and expecting them to be followed. He picked up his phone and dialed his mom's number. I stood by to listen to his side of the conversation—a repetition of what he'd said to me. Five minutes later, he hung up.

"What did she say? Did she understand?"

"She completely understood. She said she would get on the phone and talk to *all* those people—starting with Ross."

"Good."

"I'm gonna go tell Jack that I spoke to her, that she's calling all the grown-ups, and tell him what she's telling them. In light of this latest development, though, I think it's time we tell him that he's probably going to have surgery. Don't you?"

"I guess so. Let's do it tomorrow, though."

"Jule—"

"Just give me one more day, okay? One day more."

* * *

But I didn't get to wait another twenty-four hours.

On Friday afternoon, I was upstairs in my room when my cell phone rang. It was my sister-in-law.

"Sorry I wasn't able to call you back until now. I was on the road." Cathy traveled extensively on business. "Mom told me and Steve about Jack. We're so sorry."

"Thanks. I just wanted to talk. I guess you can relate to what we're going through."

"Oh, yeah. I know it's hard. How's Jack doing?"

"He's doing okay, but we haven't told him everything yet. I mean, he's aware that he's going to have a biopsy..." I gave her an abbreviated, facts-only version of our conference with Pat, and described the O'Barrs' efforts to help us find a surgeon.

"It might take a little time," she said, "but I know you'll find the right one, and I'm sure he will advise you. I'd say, if possible, try to skip the biopsy, especially if he's going to have surgery anyway."

"She did say the surgeon might choose to skip it, and just have the tumor itself analyzed by the pathologists. It's just that I don't know how we're going to tell Jack that he's going to have to have brain surgery. He's doing so well right now—he's almost 100 percent recovered from the shunt surgery. I think he's going to be crushed if he finds out now that he has to go back on the table..." My voice cracked and tears welled up in my eyes.

"I know it's not something you're looking forward to, Julie. But we know a woman here in Winston-Salem who also had a brain tumor. She had surgery about three weeks ago, and she's doing fine. I just saw her at a soccer game sitting with the other parents and cheering the team."

Hearing about someone else's good fortune was nice, but it didn't directly affect my boy. "That's good to know."

"Try not to worry. Doctors can do amazing things."

I wiped away a tear. "Thanks for your support, Cathy. We'll keep you guys posted."

"Hang in there. We're praying for you."

I hung up and collected myself, opened the bedroom door to go back downstairs, and stopped short.

Jack was two steps away from me in the hall.

He was on his knees. "Mom! I was going to my room and I overheard my name—"

I put my hands on his shoulders. "Jack—"

"'If he finds out now he has to go back on the table'?"

Oh God. This was not the way I wanted him to find out. I felt as if I'd just slapped his face. My heart was racing. How could I undo this?

"Mom! Is it true—what you said? Do I have to have brain surgery?" His eyes were full of panic and his body tense.

"The doctor told all of us about the biopsy—"

"I know, but I thought—I didn't think—"

I pulled him to his feet and looked up at his eyes, now full of tears. He was shaking. "Honey, I'm so sorry you found out this way. Dad and I were going to talk to you about it tonight. We're not sure of anything yet, but it looks like you *are* going to have to have surgery. We talked to a doctor from Emory that the O'Barrs know, and that's what she said. But you may not need a biopsy first. When Dad gets home, let's sit down together and talk about everything, okay?"

He let out a deep breath. "Okay."

"You know the O'Barrs are helping us find a doctor. We're waiting to see if any of them will agree to look at the MRI and then give us a call. After that, we'll figure out what to do."

"Oh, Mom."

I reached my arms around him and gave him a hug. "We're gonna get through this, baby. Dad and I will be with you, every step of the way. I promise."

Chapter 6

June 4 - 16

There was another life that I might have had,
but I am having this one.

– Kazuo Ishiguro

That night, Dennis and I sat down to talk to Jack. We told him about our visit with Pat, only leaving out her opinion that the tumor might not be a germinoma.

"Bottom line, Jack," Dennis said, "she said that surgery is the only way to get you healed. You know about all the hospitals we're contacting. We'll go wherever we need to go, whether they'll agree to talk to us on the phone first, or not."

"When?"

"It depends on what the doctors say," I said. "Probably soon, though."

Jack shook his head slightly. "I know this is the least of my problems, but the last day of my internship is June twenty-fifth."

"That's three weeks from today," I said. "But let's not worry about the timing yet. Hopefully, we'll hear from Johns Hopkins and Duke soon. I'll see what M.D. Anderson says when I call."

"What about San Francisco?" asked Jack.

"We found out today that they won't do a phone conference," said Dennis. "We'd have to make a trip out there."

"Go all the way out there, without knowing whether they can even help me?"

"I believe they could help," I said, "but we wouldn't be able to talk to them on the telephone before we went."

"I don't want to do that," said Jack. "I mean, not if I don't have to. I think we should wait for Duke and Johns Hopkins, and see what M.D. Anderson says."

"Okay," said Dennis.

I nodded. "I agree."

Jack cocked his head. "What about Emory?"

"Pat wasn't sure it was the best place for you," said Dennis. "She said they don't see that many brain tumors."

"Okay," said Jack. "Forget Emory."

* * *

The next day, Jack slept late and drove to Athens in the afternoon, promising to text me when he got there. I spent the weekend trying to distract myself by reading. Late Sunday afternoon, he was back home and ready to get back to work the next day. That night, as usual, after watching another episode of *Lost*, we talked in his room before he went to sleep.

He stretched out under the covers and I sat down on the edge of the bed.

"Mom, do you think we'll know something this week? I mean, do you think we'll hear from the rest of the doctors?"

I was relieved that he'd started to accept the inevitable. "I imagine we will. I hope so."

"Me, too. It's just—"

"What?"

"How soon do you think I'll have to have this surgery?"

"I don't know. First we have to hear from them. I'm thinking the earliest the surgery could happen is next week."

"I hope it isn't until after the twenty-fifth."

"Let's not worry about it until after we talk to the doctors, and we decide where we're going. Maybe it can happen the week after the twenty-fifth."

"But we go to Texas on July third. Maybe I can wait and have it the week after we get back."

I looked away for a second, then back at his eyes. I knew what I needed to say, but I didn't relish adding to his woes. "Maybe. But remember how it took almost five weeks for you to recover from the shunt surgery?"

He paused and looked down. "You're saying, if I wait, I won't be recovered from this one until the middle of August?"

"Well, possibly, yeah." We both knew that classes at the University of Georgia started about that time.

He looked up. "I guess that would be cutting it close."

I nodded, and then hesitated for a second. "You do wanna go back to school this fall, right?"

"Of course I do! I don't wanna take the semester off!"

"I don't want you to, either, if you don't have to." I braced for his reaction to my next words. "But it may come down to a choice between doing that and going to Texas for vacation. I mean, as far as timing."

If everything went well, and if the doctor said he could go back to school—at all.

"But I don't wanna miss vacation, Mom! I don't want to miss seeing everybody in Texas, and going to Choctaw!"

In recent years, some of the McDermott relatives took a day trip during the week to go to the casino in Oklahoma. Jack loved going with them and playing Texas hold'em poker. "Honey, if we do miss it, we'll go visit everybody for Thanksgiving or something. Maybe you can go to Choctaw then."

He dropped his eyes, wiping away tears with one hand.

"Come on," I said. "I know you're upset, and you'll miss seeing all your cousins, but we have to get you well. If we can't go to Texas, we can't go. Let's just focus on the present. Let's wait until we hear from the doctors and decide which one we're going to. Then we'll know a lot more, okay?"

"Okay. It just hurts knowing that I probably won't be able to go to Texas. I was just starting to feel like myself again over the last couple of weeks. Now I'm gonna have to go through another surgery and recovery all over again, and I know it's gonna be worse this time."

I grabbed his hand. "You know what? You can *do* it. All we have to do is find the right doctor."

"Gosh, Mom." He sighed. "I had a whole different plan for what I was going to do this summer. I was gonna hang out with my friends in Atlanta, go to Athens, go to Texas, and play golf."

I gave him a weak, apologetic smile. "I know. You can still do some stuff you wanna do. You've got your job, and so far, the schedule has worked out. You went to Athens, and you've hung out with your friends a couple times."

He sighed. Tears brimmed in his eyes. I squeezed his hand.

"Jack, we have to focus on getting you well again. I know you're upset about vacation, and I know it isn't easy. But we've got to do whatever it takes to get you well. We're not taking 'no' for an answer, remember?" My eyes were misty.

"Okay. I love you, Mom."

"I love you, too." I gave him a hug and said goodnight.

Minutes later, I was in bed next to Dennis. I gave him a summary of my conversation with Jack.

"Did he get it—that we aren't going to Texas?"

"Yeah, but he's pretty sad. And he wants to finish the internship. Dennis, I just wish I could make all of this go away."

"So do I." He pulled me closer. "I'm glad he went to see Jason in Athens this weekend."

We kissed each other goodnight, and I lay in bed trying to sleep. My thoughts traveled back to when I was nineteen and in college, a time when my biggest concerns were writing papers, studying for exams, and meeting boys. If I had been told one day that I had a brain tumor, my whole world would have crashed and collapsed.

I would have cried for days, if not weeks. Like Jack, I would have mourned the loss of my summer, the plans I had looked forward to. I would have felt very sorry for myself. I would have wanted to stay in my room and hide.

I wouldn't have been able to deal with the crushing blows that just seemed to keep on coming for Jack.

* * *

PHONE CALL   **June 9, 2010**

Julie McDermott called and wants to know who Dr. Tomaras uses as a contact person @ M.D. Anderson?

Please call her as she has some questions.

* * *

Jack went to work every day and occasionally volunteered at Whole World Theatre. He often went to the local YMCA to play basketball. One day, he and Brian played a round of golf. When I wasn't paying bills, doing housework, or picking out fabrics for furniture, I spent my time writing.

On Friday afternoons, I went to my writers' critique group meetings, as I had been doing for almost two years. My colleagues at the Writers' Circle had become good friends, and with Jack's okay, I had told them the basics of his situation. At our meeting on Friday, they all wrote messages on and signed a card they gave me for him. I was touched by the gesture and by their support.

In mid-June, Dr. Tomaras' contact at M.D. Anderson called and said if we wanted to talk to them, we would have to come to Houston; they were unwilling to do a phone conference first. Jack said he wanted to wait until we heard back from Johns Hopkins and Duke before we booked any trip. Early the following week, we did. Both said they would look at the MRI disk and give us a call.

My parents had stopped questioning me about Jack. My assurances that he was doing fine and was going to work each day seemed to satisfy them. I hadn't heard from either of my siblings, so I assumed they'd accepted our parents' explanation of what happened back in May. However, now that we were getting close to knowing what lay ahead, and especially because we'd kept it from them for so long, I was even more apprehensive about disclosing the truth to Mom and Dad.

They'd be shocked and upset that we hadn't told them earlier. They might not understand why we hadn't—no, they definitely wouldn't understand, and I didn't want to try to explain. But they were entitled to their feelings and to their reaction to the news. I couldn't get upset with them about the way they dealt with it. If they got mad that I had delayed telling them, there was nothing I could do. What was done was done.

On Wednesday evening, June 16, Dennis was outside watering his tomatoes and Jack was watching TV in the den when our home telephone rang. He picked it up.

"Yes, this is Jack McDermott."

Clutching a dish towel, I stepped in from the kitchen and sat down on the sofa. Jack nodded at me. "Hello, Dr. Friedman."

I listened as he spoke with Dr. Allan Friedman, the neuro-surgeon-in-chief at Duke University Hospital—the same doctor who had operated on Ted Kennedy.

"Yes," Jack said. "I'm nineteen. I just finished my freshman year at the University of Georgia."

I leaned forward while Jack talked for a few moments about his life. He paused to listen, then spoke again.

"Well, it all started when I had problems reading my final exams. When I got home, I went to an eye doctor and then had an MRI, and that's when they found it."

I studied his face for the next few minutes while he described his blurred and double vision, and as he listened again while the doctor spoke.

"Sure, that's fine. My mom's right here." He handed me the phone.

"Hello?" My throat felt dry.

"Hello, Mrs. McDermott. Dr. Allan Friedman here."

"Thank you for calling, Dr. Friedman."

"You're welcome. Your son sounds like a very nice young man."

"He is." I smiled at Jack. My heart was pounding.

"Well, he and I have talked about his tumor, and I told him that I'd like to see him and talk about how to treat it. He seems to think that would be a good idea. Do you think you can make the trip up here to Durham?"

"Certainly, we could."

"Good. Have you ever been up here?"

"Yes, we have. My husband and I are graduates of UNC, so we've visited the area a lot over the years—though we're more familiar with Chapel Hill than Durham."

He chuckled. "Oh, so you're Tar Heels. I'm sure you'll feel right at home up here, then. My wife is a physician and a professor over at UNC, and does research at the hospital. Our daughter goes to Duke, but one of our sons is in school over there in Chapel Hill. I love UNC, except for when Duke plays them in basketball!"

I smiled. The UNC connection was welcome, though of course not necessary. The doctor switched to the subject of his call, said he had viewed Jack's MRI, and felt there was no need for a biopsy. "Not only that, but it's too risky, anyway," he said. "What we need to do is to remove the tumor. If you decide to come to see me, next week looks open. I could operate on Jack next Wednesday, June the twenty-third, with a consultation appointment the previous day, on Tuesday."

"Okay," I said. I glanced at Jack. A question popped into my head. Should I ask it? This might be my only chance. I cleared my throat. "Dr. Friedman, I'm just wondering—is it possible to wait one more week? That is, do it the following Tuesday and Wednesday? I mean, would that be all right for Jack, and will it work for you?"

Dr. Friedman paused for a second. "Well, I suppose so. Why, though?"

"If it doesn't work, we could definitely come on the twenty-second. It's just that, about two weeks after his shunt surgery, Jack started a five-week internship, and his last day is next Friday, the twenty-fifth."

"Hmm. What kind of internship is it?"

"It's an acting internship in a drama camp for high school kids. On the last day, they have a performance, and all of our family is invited to it."

"That sounds like fun. So is Jack an actor? Is he in plays?"

"He was, in high school. This past year, he tried out for a few roles at UGA and joined an improv group," I babbled. "He even thought about majoring in Theatre, but I think he's changed his mind. He's decided to apply to the Business School and major in Finance."

"Very good plan. Well, tell you what. I'll give you the name and number of my scheduler, and you tell him that Dr. Friedman said to make a consultation appointment for Tuesday, June twenty-ninth. Unless there's something going on that I don't know about, that should be fine. Will you and your husband be coming in to see me with Jack?"

"Yes. Maybe we'll drive up on that Monday. We'll need to find a hotel near the hospital."

"My scheduler can help you with all of that. He'll give you some recommendations. Anyway, when we meet that Tuesday, I'll examine Jack and we'll discuss everything. If he chooses to go ahead and have the surgery performed here, we could admit him that day, and do it the following morning."

"Okay."

"Once we remove his tumor, we'll have our pathologists analyze it. Then, we'll talk about whatever follow-up treatment he may need. Pathology will take a few days, and for that and a few other reasons, we'll need for you all to stay up here in Durham for about seven to ten days. Can you plan on that?"

"Yes." I looked at Jack, who was watching me.

"Mrs. McDermott, we'll talk about this when you come in, but in case you're wondering, I want to let you know that I do this type of surgery all the time. I just operated on a twenty-year-old man a few weeks ago with a very similar presentation to your son's. Everything went very well, and that young man is doing great. So don't worry, and I'll see all of you very soon. If you've got a pen, I'll go ahead and give you that name and number to call to make the consultation appointment."

"Great." I stepped over to my desk. "Go ahead, Doctor."

Chapter 7

June 16 - 25

"You never really understand a person until you consider
things from his point of view...
Until you climb inside of his skin and walk around in it."

– Harper Lee, *To Kill a Mockingbird*

Jack and I told Dennis about our conversations with Dr. Friedman, and Dennis agreed that we should make an appointment at Duke on the twenty-ninth and drive up to North Carolina the day before.

"I'm so glad he called and talked to me," said Jack. "I feel a lot better about everything now."

"We haven't heard from Johns Hopkins yet," I said. "I thought you wanted to wait to hear from them also."

Jack cocked his head. "I do. But in the meantime, I think we should go ahead with the plan to see Dr. Friedman."

"I agree," said Dennis.

When we went to bed, Dennis told me he was surprised that the famous neurosurgeon had called our home at night.

"I was, too. I'm glad he did, though."

He gave me a quizzical look. "It just sounds like he was really interested in getting Jack to come up there."

"What do you mean?"

"Well, like, he knew that he could help him. Which is great. On the other hand, if Dr. Allan Friedman is calling you at night, telling you he wants to operate on you, that says it's a pretty serious situation."

"Which we already knew," I said.

"Right."

"Well, in any case, I was glad he told me about having recently operated on a twenty-year-old guy with the same thing. It makes me feel a little better."

"Me, too." Dennis pulled me close to him. "We'll get through this together, Jule."

"I love you, babe."

"I love you, too."

I closed my eyes. Jack's surgery was about to be added to Dr. Allan Friedman's schedule. I pictured my boy in a hospital gown being rolled into an operating room, and felt a sense of dread tinged with relief. But I pushed the vision away.

* * *

On Thursday morning, I asked Jack if I could let my dear friend and college roommate Alison know what was going on, now that we had a plan. Alison lived in northern California and had visited us a couple of times in recent years. Jack was fine with telling her. I got in touch with her, and after an email exchange, we planned to talk the next morning, her time.

Then, at 1:00, I met my friends Patty and Suzanne for lunch at Nordstrom's Cafe.

Jack had been friends with Patty's son Josh and Suzanne's son Conor since fourth grade. Suzanne's family was from Ireland, but had lived in the U.S. for many years, most recently as our neighbors down the street. They had moved back to Ireland, and Suzanne was in town for a visit right now, staying with Patty. With Jack's permission, I'd told them about him on the phone.

We paid for our lunch and sat down at a table in the back.

"Oh, Julie," said Suzanne, "if you want to talk about it—"

"I do." Over the next few minutes, I updated her and Patty, ending with our decision to make an appointment at Duke with Dr. Friedman. Somewhere in there, I described the episode of Jack finding out he was going to need another surgery by overhearing my telephone conversation with my sister-in-law.

"What a way for him to find out," said Patty.

"I know," I said. "It was awful."

Suzanne's eyes were soft. "I'm so sorry. How's he doing?"

"Okay. Thank God he has this acting internship going on. I'm glad he gets to finish it and won't miss their performance on the last day."

"What day is it?" asked Patty.

"Next Friday."

"When is the trip to Texas?" asked Suzanne.

"It's the week of the Fourth, but we can't go. Jack was upset when we talked about it, but he understood that if we postpone the surgery, he may not be able to go back to school this fall."

"But even if you don't postpone it, *will* he be able to go back?" asked Suzanne.

"I don't know. It's not a given."

Patty gave me an empathetic look. "I'm so sorry you're going through this, Julie. Poor Jack. What a thing to happen."

"You know what, though, Julie?" Suzanne looked directly into my eyes. "He's young, and he's strong. The best doctors in the world are right here in the United States. I'm glad he's going to Dr. Friedman. Jack's going to get through this, I just know he is."

"Yes, he will," said Patty. "As far as school goes, you can't think that far ahead right now."

"I know," I said.

"And even if he doesn't get to go back this fall, that's okay. He may need a few months of recovery. A friend of a friend of mine has a nephew who had a brain tumor, and he had surgery, too. Over the next six months, he had to learn to walk and to talk again, but he did, and now he's doing much, much better."

I looked at Patty with fear in my eyes. I hadn't even considered such possibilities. I burst into tears.

"Julie," said Suzanne, her voice firm. She reached for my arm. "That's not going to happen. Don't lose hope. Jack's going to be okay."

* * *

On Friday morning, Alison and I had a long talk. I brought her up to date and described everything, from the beginning. She offered her support and prayers, and afterward I felt comforted and a little bit less alone.

That afternoon, I was sitting at a table in the Borders Bookstore cafe, listening to a writer friend read his work at our critique group meeting, when my cell phone rang. I looked at the screen. It showed a number I didn't recognize with a 410 area code.

"Sorry," I mouthed as I stood and backed away toward a bookshelf. "Hello?"

"Hello, this is Dr. Jon Weingart calling from Johns Hopkins Hospital. Is this Mrs. McDermott?"

"It is. Thank you for calling, Doctor."

"It's my pleasure. I wanted to let you know that I've seen your son Jack's MRI disk that was sent to me through your internist, a Dr. Thomas O'Barr?"

"Yes?"

"Dr. O'Barr said in his note that you're sending the disk out to a few other neurosurgeons around the country."

"That's correct."

"Well, I'm not sure where you are in the process, but I'd be happy to discuss Jack's case with you now, that is, if you have a few minutes?"

"Yes, of course." I leaned against the bookshelf and took a deep breath.

We spoke for about fifteen minutes. Dr. Weingart's opinion was identical to the one expressed by Dr. Friedman: a biopsy was too risky, and surgery to remove the tumor was absolutely necessary. Dr. Weingart said he did this kind of surgery frequently, and asked me if we had talked with any other neurosurgeons.

"We spoke to Dr. Allan Friedman at Duke the other night. He talked with Jack and with me, and he said the same thing you did."

"Dr. Friedman is a top neurosurgeon—one of the best that you'll find anywhere—and Duke is a wonderful place. It's where I was trained and received my degree."

"Oh, really?"

"Yes. Mrs. McDermott, I know this is a very difficult time for you and for your family. I have a son about the same age as Jack, and I feel for you in this situation."

"Thank you so much." I choked back emotion from my voice and impulsively decided to ask a personal question—one to which I needed the answer. "Dr. Weingart, if your son had what Jack has, and so you weren't able to operate on him yourself..."

"Yes?"

"Would you ask Dr. Friedman to do it?"

"*Absolutely*, I would."

* * *

That night when he got home from work, I gave Dennis a recap of my conversation with Dr. Weingart.

"Let's sit down with Jack and tell him what he said before we go out tonight," said Dennis. We had a reservation at a favorite restaurant in Buckhead to celebrate our anniversary, which was the next day.

"Okay. I didn't ask him to call back and talk to Jack, but he gave me his email address in case we want to contact him."

"I wonder if Jack will want to make an appointment up at Johns Hopkins, too," said Dennis. "If he does, we could book a flight to Baltimore, and then he could decide where he wants to go for the surgery."

"Okay. If we wait to book an appointment with him until after the one at Duke though, that's going to delay the surgery even more."

"Tell Jack exactly what you told me. Tell him that Dr. Weingart said he trained at Duke, and tell him what he said about Dr. Friedman—"

"And that he would choose him to operate on his own son," I finished the sentence. "I mean, I guess Weingart wouldn't have said no to that question—"

"We don't know that," said Dennis. "In any case, I'm certainly willing to fly the three of us up to Baltimore to talk to the guy, if Jack wants to. But if he decides to go to the Duke appointment on the twenty-ninth and then have the surgery there, that's fine, too."

"Oh, my God. This thing is really going to happen."

"I know, babe." He put his arm around me. "Let's also talk to Jack about telling your parents. Once he decides where to go for the surgery, I think he'll be okay with it, and that he'll want to. They need to know as soon as he's ready to tell them."

* * *

Jack decided he wanted to go to the appointment with Dr. Friedman and, unless he changed his mind at the consultation, have the Duke neurosurgeon perform the surgery the following day. Plan B was to contact Dr. Weingart and ask him to do it. Jack was fine with telling my parents and siblings what was going on, now that we had made some decisions.

"But I don't want to be there when you tell Grandma and Granddad," he told me on Saturday morning. "Can you go and talk to them without me?"

"Sure. I'll ask Brian to go with me–maybe we'll take them out to lunch next week, while you're at work."

"Good idea."

"What about Aunt Pam?"

"Could you tell her after the lunch?"

"Okay. I'll call her that afternoon and fill her in. Or maybe Grandma and Granddad can do it. I'll ask them to tell Uncle Bart, too."

"Fine." Bart was six years younger than me, and he and his wife had three young sons. We had never been close and hardly ever talked on the phone, but he was frequently in touch with our parents. Pam and I kept in closer touch, but we visited only a few times a year. She was five years older than me, was single and had no children.

I waited until Wednesday to tell my folks. Just before Brian and I left for the restaurant where we'd agreed to meet for lunch, I sat down to write an email.

June 23, 2010 12:26 PM
Dear Dr. Weingart,

Please forgive me for not getting in touch with you sooner after our conversation of Friday. I am so grateful to you for looking at Jack's records, taking the time to call me and to discuss your thoughts about Jack and answer all my questions.

Jack, my husband, Dennis, and I talked about everything, and we struggled with making the right decision about where to go for the surgery that we understand is absolutely necessary for Jack. Dr. Allan Friedman had also called a day or two before I spoke to you, and he talked with Jack and me.

Jack, Dennis, and I believe that both the doctors (and the teams) at Johns Hopkins and at Duke are top quality and two of the very best in the country, and that we couldn't go wrong at either facility. We came to a decision that we believe is the right one for our family, and we made an appointment with Dr. Friedman for next Tues. We will travel there on Monday, and the surgery is to be midweek.

I also appreciate your very kind words and good wishes. If something unforeseen happens and Dr. Friedman becomes unavailable, I would be most grateful to be able to call you and ask you to treat Jack. Thank you very much,
Sincerely,

Julia McDermott
Atlanta, Georgia

* * *

"Thanks for going with me today, Brian," I said as we drove to the Bat & Ball.

"No problem, Mom."

"Tell you what. I'll bring it up, but I want you to do the talking. Okay?" I was afraid that if I started speaking, I'd lose my composure, and then we'd all start crying.

"Don't worry. I'll answer all their questions."

"Thanks, honey. I know they're going to have a lot. I'll help if I can. They won't be happy that we waited this long to tell them, but–"

"Jack didn't want to, until he knew what he was going to have to do, right?"

"Right."

"They'll understand," said Brian. "At least, Granddad will. Jack's had a lot to deal with, and during the last few weeks, he's been in his man-cave."

I smiled and pulled into a parking place. I felt comforted by his presence, and grateful that he'd agreed to explain everything. "Yeah, I guess you're right. Well, here goes." We entered the dark, cool pub and found my parents sitting side by side at a wooden booth. Brian and I slid into the bench across from them. The stained glass light fixtures overhead cast a dim glow.

"Hi," I said. "Thanks for meeting us."

"Of course," said Dad. "You told us on the phone that you wanted to bring us up to date on Jack?" His eyes were wide. "Tell us what's going on, Julie."

"Yes, tell us," said Mom.

Just then, a waiter stopped at our table, took our order, and then disappeared to get our drinks.

Mom turned to me. "Tell us! Is Jack okay?"

"Well–" I stopped and looked at Brian.

"Grandma and Granddad, Jack has a brain tumor."

"*What?*" said Mom. Her eyebrows shot up into diagonal worry lines. "What are you talking about?"

Dad looked me in the eye. "You said the surgery he had last month had to do with his vision, Julie. You didn't tell us he had a brain tumor!"

Brian raised his hand and spoke. "That surgery *was* for his vision. But his vision problem was caused by his tumor. It's behind his eyes."

"Why haven't you told us?" asked Mom.

I started to speak, then looked at Brian, who said, "Jack didn't want to tell you until he knew what was going to happen. Now he does. Next week, he's going to Duke to have another surgery to get the tumor taken out."

The waiter quietly placed our drinks on the table, then walked away.

"Brain surgery?" asked Dad. "Isn't there any other way?"

"No," said Brian. "He's got to have this done."

Dad trained his eyes on me. "You must have gotten a second opinion?"

Brian spoke up. "Mom and Dad have talked to lots of doctors over the last few weeks, and they all agreed on surgery."

"That's right," I said. "The surgeon at Northside gave us some referrals, and we've been in touch with doctors at Emory and Johns Hopkins as well."

"And they've decided to go to Duke," said Brian.

Mom turned to me. "Oh, Julie, what you must have been going through. I just can't imagine—"

I looked into her eyes. "Mom, I couldn't tell you over the phone, and I didn't think I could do it in person, either. So I asked Brian to come with me and do it."

She looked at Brian, then back at me. "Thank you, honey. Now, will you all keep us informed from now on?"

I nodded. "Dennis and Jack and I are leaving on Monday for Durham. We're staying at a hotel, and meeting with Dr. Friedman on Tuesday. The surgery will probably be the next morning."

"Have you told Pam?" asked Dad.

"Not yet," I said. "Will you guys call her, and will you tell Bart?"

"Okay," said Dad. "We'll call both of them. Don't worry about it."

Our lunch arrived, and once the waiter disappeared again, Dad spoke. "How has Jack been doing?"

"All right," said Brian. "He's been busy working–"

"Has he been feeling okay?" asked Mom.

"He's doing fine, Grandma."

"Yeah," I said. "It's great that he already had that job lined up. It started in the middle of May, and his last day is Friday. They have a big performance that morning, and we're all invited to attend. Can you go?"

"Of course!" said Mom. "We wouldn't miss it."

Dad nodded. "You just tell us when and where, and we'll be there."

I felt relieved now that Mom and Dad knew everything, and I didn't have to continue being vague. I was glad Brian was with me and that we had told them in a public place, where all of us had to keep our emotions under control, and grateful they had put aside whatever hurt feelings they had.

I was also happy that they'd agreed so quickly to come to the performance. Both had been strong supporters of Jack's acting endeavors in high school. Dad's lifelong passion was art, and I had many of his paintings and drawings hanging in my home. The four of us continued chatting as we ate our lunch. After the waiter took our plates, Mom and Brian went to the restroom and I sat facing my dad.

"Honey," he said, "I just want you to know, I understand why Jack needed some time before you told us."

"You do?"

Dad's eyes were soft. "Yes. He's the one who has to face this thing. You just tell him that we love him, and we'll do whatever we can to help him and all of you, okay?"

"Thanks." I reached for his hand. "Dad, Dennis and I have been through difficult things before, and so have you and Mom— but nothing we've ever been through has been as hard as this. Not even close. Whenever we've gotten through one challenge, though, another one always seems to come along to replace it! Dad, why can't *everything* be good at the same time?"

Dad shook his head slowly. "Honey. That's not life. That's called heaven."

* * *

On Friday morning, we were up early to go to Decatur to see the performance. Dennis was taking the morning off and planned to go to his downtown office after the show. Mom and Dad were meeting us there, and Jack was driving his own car.

I checked my email just before we left and found a new message.

June 24, 2010 10:32 PM
Julia,

That is great. Duke is a great place. If we can help in any way at Hopkins, let us know.

Jon Weingart

I told Dennis about it in the car. "That was a nice email," he said.

"It was." I sipped my coffee. Brian and Annette were silent in the back seat. Thirty minutes later, we pulled into the church parking lot and entered the building through a side door.

Mom and Dad sat waiting for us in the second row, and Dennis, Annette, and I filled in the empty seats next to them. Brian took a seat behind us, and a few minutes later Jack's friend Brendan O'Barr came in and sat down next to him.

I turned around. "Hi, Brendan! I'm so glad you could make it!"

He smiled. "Hello, Mrs. McDermott. I wouldn't miss it."

We chatted for a few minutes until a stylishly dressed, forty-something woman walked in and faced the audience.

"Thank you all for coming today, and welcome to this per-formance of Atlanta Street Theatre," she said. "My name is Nevaina Rhodes, and I'm the person in charge of this year's camp." She described the camp and what the college interns had been doing with the middle school and high school kids. They'd written, directed and practiced original skits—scenes—they were about to perform. The show was titled "Life, Death and the DASH in Between," and it would reflect the things that were go-ing on in the actors' lives.

"Ladies and gentlemen," said Nevaina, "before we begin, I want to tell you a little about one of our college interns, Jack McDermott."

Dennis and I exchanged glances. Had Jack told her or any-one here about his tumor, and about his surgery next week?

"Jack is an extraordinary young man," said Nevaina. "He just finished his freshman year at the University of Georgia. Then he showed up here for work, two weeks after he had emergency brain surgery. You'll recognize him right away: he's the real tall guy with the real short haircut." She smiled broadly, paused and surveyed the room. "Jack has worked so hard and has been so dedicated over the last five weeks, always with a smile and a positive attitude. He's been an inspiration to all of us here at Atlanta Street Theatre, and we've been fortunate to have him. I just can't say enough about him. Let's all give him a hand."

The audience applauded, and I looked at Dennis and then at my parents, who were beaming with pride.

"Wow. I wish Jack could have heard her," I whispered to Dennis.

"Maybe he did—maybe he's right behind the curtain."

We later learned that he hadn't heard Nevaina. He had been backstage getting ready, and his first appearance wasn't until a quarter of an hour later. He played several roles in the short scenes that followed. In one, he was the husband of a very sick wife; in another (called "Drip, Drip, Buzz"), he was on a cot in the preoperative room of a hospital. A (fake) IV was attached to his arm, and a small heartbeat monitor sounded behind him. In yet another, he was in a group of kids and telling a story, each of them trying to win a "pity party" contest. At the end of that scene, he stood and faced the audience, pointed at his close-cropped head and scar, and proclaimed that he had won the contest: he had survived a brain tumor.

Survived?

My father, my mother, Dennis and I turned towards one another and exchanged apprehensive glances. Jack knew he hadn't survived it—yet. The skits were supposed to be fictional, but also give clues about the kids' lives. Evidently, Jack hadn't told his whole story to the people here. He'd led them to believe that the surgery he'd had in May was the way he had "survived" a brain tumor. My stomach clenched at this realization, and at what he hadn't been truthful about—not because I disapproved of his decision, but because I felt anxious. My fierce faith that he was going to live—that we weren't taking 'no' for an answer—was momentarily shaken.

As all the kids and interns piled onstage for the finale, I had the distinct impression that they believed Jack was now well. And for him, it wasn't about winning a pity party contest. It was about winning the fight that he knew loomed ahead of him. What he needed was for others to believe he had already won it—so that he could believe he would live.

When the show was over, Dennis and I congratulated Jack on his performance. Then we had to leave so I could drive Dennis to the MARTA station. We didn't get a chance to thank Nevaina for her kind words about Jack, but I made a mental note to do it later. Annette, Brian, and Jack went with my parents to Manuel's Tavern, an Atlanta landmark located right around the corner, for a celebratory lunch. I met everyone there, and the six of us sat at a round table and gave the waiter our orders. Jack had invited Brendan, but he'd had to get back to his summer job.

Everyone complimented Jack on his performance and listened to his funny stories about working at the drama camp. I was relieved that no one at the table asked why he hadn't told them he was going to Duke next week, or why he let them believe he had already survived the tumor.

When Jack went to the men's room, my dad turned to me. "Maybe the surgery that he already had was all he was able to share."

I nodded. "I guess so. When he started this internship, his head had just been shaved and everybody could see his scar."

"You know, that's okay," said Dad. I thought the knowledge that Jack had hidden the truth from his coworkers gave Dad a little comfort about us having done the same with him and Mom. Maybe it at least softened the blow.

"Julie," said Mom, "have you talked to Pam?"

"Not yet."

"Well, you need to call her," she said. "She's worried."

"I will this weekend. You guys told her we were going to Duke, right?"

Dad nodded. "But give her a call."

"Okay."

"What a wonderful show," said Dad as Jack made his way back to the table. "I'm so glad we were all there to see you on stage!"

* * *

Jack and I talked in his room again that evening before bed. After we chatted about the show for a while, I asked if he would mind if I emailed my Bible study group before we left for North Carolina, to ask for their prayers.

"I'll tell them not to tell anybody, to keep it to themselves," I said, "but I'd like to tell them what's going on. They all *will* pray for you, and all of us."

"Okay," said Jack. "As long as we aren't talking about the whole church."

"It's just a small group–about fifteen women. At most."

"Fine. Did you talk to Aunt Pam today?"

"Yeah. She wanted us to talk to a doctor at Johns Hopkins that one of her friends recommended. I told her we had already talked to Dr. Weingart up there." I didn't tell Jack that she had peppered me with questions about what might have caused Jack's tumor, such as whether he had spent too much time playing video games when he was little. Nor did I tell him that she'd given me unsolicited advice.

"Is Dr. Weingart the one her friend said to talk to?"

"No. I think it was a radiation oncologist, but I'm sure they work together. The doctors at Johns Hopkins probably all work as a team, just like Dr. Friedman said they do at Duke."

"Oh. Mom, now that this thing is about to happen..."

"What?"

He sucked in his breath. "I'm scared."

"I know. But it's going to be okay. We're going to see one of the very best doctors in the world."

"Still."

I reached for his hand. "We're *with* you, no matter what. Remember, we're not taking 'no' for an answer." Since the first time I'd said it, it had become a catch phrase for us–a way, I thought, to try and keep hope alive and fear at bay.

He wiped a tear away. "Okay, Mom. I love you."

* * *

In bed, I thought about my conversation with Pam. Even though I told her we'd gotten more than one opinion, she had urged me to reconsider our decision to go to Duke. She had emphasized that her friend strongly advised making an appointment with the on-cologist he knew at Hopkins first. I had tried to tell her about my conversation with Dr. Weingart there, and about our earlier talk with Dr. Friedman.

Perhaps she thought we'd made a hasty decision to go to North Carolina because it was closer. But when I tried to explain our reasons, she had cut me off and argued, insisting that we take her advice. Without much choice, I let her talk until she was through, thanked her, and gently repeated that we had made our decision.

I knew she had the best intentions and that she sincerely wanted to help; she was probably in shock, having just found out the truth. But she had acted as if the reason we told her was so that I could ask her what to do. Her assumption that I wanted her to fix things wasn't helpful, and I told her so. Our conversation went on a bit too long, and what could have been a chance for closeness and support between us had turned into a tense altercation.

I hung up feeling even more emotionally drained and hurt. I told Dennis about it, and we decided not to tell Jack. Instead of questioning our judgment, I'd just wanted Pam to listen to me without interrupting, and to trust that we had sought opinions from other doctors. I hadn't wanted her to advise us or to doubt our decisions. I'd wanted her to come into my world for a few minutes and to show empathy for what I was going through, as some of my close friends had done. I'd wanted her to step outside of who she was, out of her older-sister self, her priorities and impulses, and even her personality—to be there for me and support me in my grief. I'd wished I could have talked to her about what I was going through, and that I could have shared my deepest feelings.

But I couldn't. I had to hold them inside.

Chapter 8

June 26 - 29

Courage is resistance to fear, mastery of fear —
not absence of fear.

— Mark Twain

I kept busy that weekend and tried not to think about what was about to happen.

I made a reservation at the Millennium Hotel in Durham. It was one of the hotels on a list that Dr. Friedman's scheduler had sent, and it was close to the hospital. If Jack decided to go ahead and have the surgery at Duke, then we would stay in Durham for a week or more.

Dennis had been updating his mother over the last few weeks and he told her what we had decided about the vacation. Brian and Annette were going, as planned, on July 3. Elen and Mark offered to take them to the airport on Saturday.

"Thank you so much," I told Elen on the phone.

"You're so welcome. Don't give it a thought."

"I could have asked my parents to take them, but they're kind of fragile right now."

"Don't worry about it. You just focus on Jack. Call me whenever you want, and remember, you're all in our prayers."

I called Dad to let him know they had a ride. "Hopefully, we'll be back before they get home."

"Okay. If not, and you need us to pick them up, call me."

"I will. Thanks, Dad."

On Monday morning, June 28, Dennis, Jack and I left Atlanta for the six-hour drive to Durham. We arrived that afternoon, checked into the hotel and hung out in our room until time for dinner. That night, we got ready for bed early and watched television. Jack stretched out on one of the queen-sized beds, and Dennis and I did the same on the other. When we turned off the TV and the lights, I lay next to Dennis and listened as Jack tossed and turned in bed.

After a little while, he whispered, "Mom, are you asleep?"

"No."

"Is Dad?"

Dennis grunted. I said, "Almost. Why?"

"Can we go talk in the bathroom? I don't want to wake Dad."

"Okay."

We traipsed over to the bathroom. I turned on the light and shut the door.

"What is it, honey?"

He looked down at me. Tears filled his eyes. "It's just—I'm really, really scared, Mom. I know this has to happen, and that it's the only way I'm going to get well. But I'm afraid."

I grabbed his arm. "Oh, honey. I am, too."

"You are?"

"Yeah. But it would be weird if we weren't afraid."

He sighed. "Still, though."

I moved my hand to his and held it. "Let's not think too far ahead, okay? We're meeting with Dr. Friedman tomorrow morning, and when we do, he's going to explain everything. We'll know a lot more then."

"Yeah, I guess you're right."

"One step at a time, okay?"

"Okay. But, Mom, I've never been so scared." A tear streamed down his face.

"It's okay for us to be afraid, Jack. But we have each other, and we're going to get through this. I know we are."

I gave him a hug and my own tears began to flow. This six-foot four-inch young man was my little boy, and he needed me. He had been a darling baby and a sweet son, and I'd always tried to protect him. When he was young, I could take care of him and keep him from harm—I could kiss away his tears. But now, as we cried together, I couldn't make everything all better.

He wiped his eyes. "I guess I'll try to go to sleep now."

"Okay."

"I love you, Mom."

"I love you too, Jack."

I turned out the bathroom light and we tiptoed to our beds. I snuggled up to Dennis, said a silent prayer, and listened to Jack breathing until he fell asleep.

* * *

After breakfast, we drove the few miles to the parking deck next to the Duke Clinic. From there, we followed the signs to the building and walked through a long pedestrian bridge. I could see the hospital building in the distance off to the right, connected to the Clinic. Construction workers were busy on the ground below between us and the hospital, their machinery clanging. Jack ambled along beside Dennis and me as we made our way through the passageway to the Clinic.

"I'm glad we gave ourselves some extra time," said Dennis. "This place is huge."

It took a good twenty minutes to get to the right place—the Brain Cancer Clinic. The three of us waited behind a sign that read: "STOP Please wait here for next available representative." When one became free, we approached the counter and Jack checked in with a male assistant.

"Mrs. McDermott?" he said. "Did you get a call this morning about the copayment?"

"Yes. I handled it on the phone with whoever it was."

"Good." He looked at his computer screen. "I just wanted to verify that."

Our bank account had been charged over two thousand dollars, and we knew that was only the beginning. We had good benefits with Dennis' employer, SunTrust, and I was glad we had a health savings account set up with enough funds in it to reimburse us. I wondered what the final bill would be, then pushed away the thought. We would figure that out and how to pay it later.

We sat down in the windowless waiting room. Other patients of various ages and stages of illness—and their families—surrounded us. I tried to gauge Jack's thoughts, being in their midst. He knew he was seriously ill, but he didn't look sick, and he said he felt fine.

The square florescent ceiling lights cast a glare over the room and no artwork dotted the drab, tan walls. This place was quite different from our pediatrician's cheery waiting room, decorated with bright posters and colorful paintings. Here, gray chairs lined up in facing rows, their shiny wood armrests snug against each other. I looked down at the carpet, made up of patterned tiles in neutral colors. The furnishings and decor in this room were identical to those in the others we had passed on our way down the corridor—all of them cancer clinics for other body parts. The signs announcing their specialties had looked menacing, their bold capital letters austere and stern.

As we waited for Jack to be summoned, I held Dennis' hand. It felt warm and protective around my cold one, like a small shield against pinpricks of despair. After a few minutes, a nurse called Jack's name. The three of us stood and followed her to an exam room, stopping on the way so she could get his height and weight. Another nurse took his vital signs and advised us that Dr. Friedman would be in shortly. Dennis and I sank into plastic chairs and Jack sat on the exam table.

This was it. We were about to meet Duke's chief of neuro-surgery, one of the top brain surgeons in the world, to talk about what to do about the tumor sitting behind Jack's eyes.

Dr. Allan Friedman entered the room, introduced himself, and shook our hands. I'd seen his photo online, and he looked just like it, with thick dark hair and a mustache. Wire-rimmed glasses perched on his nose, framing kind, thoughtful eyes, and he stood a few inches under six feet tall. He chatted with us for a few moments and then got right to his patient, examining Jack's eyes and testing his reflexes. When he was finished, the doctor sat on a stool.

"You know, Jack," he said, "the kind of surgery we do nowadays for tumors like the one you have—it hasn't always been around. Thirty years ago, it didn't exist." He waited for Jack's re-action, then glanced at Dennis and me. "In other words, if one of your parents had had what you have when they were your age, there would have been only one outcome: death."

Jack's eyes were wide and unblinking. I grabbed Dennis' hand.

"Now," continued the doctor, "I'm not saying this to scare you. I'm just telling you the truth. But the great thing is, we do have this surgery today, and it's been done for some time. Surgery is the only way to fix what you have—to get you healed and well again. You'll have to decide whether you want to go through with it. Your parents can't do that for you. So I've got to be honest with you. If you *don't* have the surgery, you'll probably be dead in a little more than a year."

Jack stared at him. "But—I feel fine."

"That's good. You've recovered very well from the surgery to place your shunt. And without surgery to remove your tumor, you'll continue to feel fine, for a while. Then, very quickly perhaps, you won't. I'm sorry that this is the way it is. Even though we've come a long way in medicine, there's just no way to treat your illness other than through surgery. Would you like me to explain what I do during it, and what you could expect?"

Jack nodded. My heart was racing.

"It takes about four hours. We put you to sleep first, and we monitor you the whole time: your heart rate, your every breath. We have a whole team that works together to take care of you. We use the best instruments and equipment, and we're very, *very* careful. We make a long incision in the back of your head, about this long," he paused and stretched his palm, "and then we take a piece of your skull out and set it aside."

I recoiled. I didn't want to imagine this, but I knew that Jack—and we—had to hear it.

"Okay," said Jack. "Go on."

Dr. Friedman looked directly into his eyes. "Then we remove your tumor. I won't describe the process in detail, but I'll tell you that it takes a while. With your tumor sitting where it is, behind your optic nerves, we're going to be extra cautious when we get to the cells located very near them."

Jack started. "What do you mean? What could happen?"

"Nothing will happen to your sight—we'll make sure of that. What I mean is, because we're being cautious, we may not be able to get all the tiny microscopic tumor cells located very close to your optic nerves. If we can't get them all, we'll talk afterward about what to do about it. We should be able to remove the vast majority of the tumor, though. Once we're done, we put the piece of your skull back where it was, fasten it with titanium screws, and close your incision."

My hand flew to my mouth. I felt dizzy and light-headed, as if I were about to pass out.

"Don't worry, Mrs. McDermott," said Dr. Friedman, looking my way. "Jack will be fine with those screws in his head." He looked back at his patient. "They'll stay in there for the rest of your life. But they won't cause you any problems. You can even go through airport security and you won't set off any alarms."

Jack gave a weak smile.

Dr. Friedman continued. "You'll have several stitches in the back of your head, and they'll stay in for a week or so. When you get back to Atlanta, you can have your family doctor remove them. When you wake up from surgery, you'll have a big bandage around your head, but you won't feel much discomfort there. You *will* have some ache and pain in your neck, and we'll give you pain medication for it. But it will be important to move your head and neck around as soon as you are able. We'll help you do that, and we'll get you up and around. We'll also ask you a lot of questions to make sure your brain is working just fine."

"What if it isn't?" asked Jack, voicing my own concern.

"It will be," said the doctor. "I feel very, very good about that. We are really good what we do."

Jack took a deep breath and let it out. "So, when does this happen?"

Dr. Friedman smiled. "We have you on the schedule for tomorrow morning, so if you decide to do it, you'll be admitted to the hospital this afternoon and will spend the night here. The surgery will take place early in the morning. You'll be done and in your room tomorrow afternoon."

"How long will he stay in the hospital?" asked Dennis.

"A few days," said the doctor. "Probably until Friday or Saturday. As I said to Mrs. McDermott on the phone, though, you'll need to stay somewhere local for about a week after that, in case of any post-surgery complications. I don't envision that in Jack's case, however."

"We're staying at a hotel close to the hospital, and can stay there until it's okay to go home," I said.

"Good. Now, Jack, about the tumor again. Once we remove it, we send it to our pathologists. They'll analyze and identify it—they'll tell us what kind of tumor it is. Then we'll know a lot more. But that process takes about a week. So, I'd say, probably by the middle of next week, we should have the results. A biopsy would have accomplished the same thing, but with only a small portion of the tumor, and as I said earlier, doing that first would just add to the risk. And it's unnecessary. Even if we did a biopsy, we'd still need to remove the tumor surgically. So doing a biopsy is out. Once we get that tumor out of your brain, you can start getting better."

Jack took another deep breath and let it out. "Okay. Let's do it."

I squeezed Dennis' hand. Dr. Friedman bid us goodbye for now, adding that a team of nurses and administrators would soon be in to take us through the process, have Jack sign authorization forms, and answer any questions. Then he left the room.

Jack stood, walked over to me, and gave me a silent hug. Dennis reached over and placed his hand on Jack's shoulder. Then Jack turned and hugged his dad.

"You okay?" asked Dennis, his eyes watery.

"Yeah."

"I like Dr. Friedman, don't you, Julie?" said Dennis.

"Yeah," I managed to say.

"He's upfront with everything," said Dennis. "He sure doesn't beat around the bush."

"No," said Jack, stepping back. "He explained everything pretty well."

"Don't worry, Jack," said Dennis. "Dr. Friedman is one of the best neurosurgeons in the world. That's why we're here. I think you've made the right decision."

Just then a medical assistant entered the room with consent forms for the surgery and privacy and insurance authorization forms. Jack skimmed them and signed his name on each.

"This last one, you may want to read through," said the assistant. "It's about whether you'd like to donate your blood and tissue to a research study."

Jack gave the man a look. "What do you mean?"

The assistant began to explain, and Jack's expression changed from curious to apprehensive. "If I sign, what happens to my tissue and blood?"

The assistant started to respond, but Dennis cut him off. "Just sign it, Jack," he said. "They use it to help other people."

"But Dad–"

"Look," said Dennis. "Don't worry about what happens to it. You ought to sign. Just do it." I gazed at Dennis, his authoritarian-dad expression masking his stress.

Jack paused, pen in hand. This was the first time either of us had ordered him to sign a consent form. After a moment, he grimaced, and a look of defeat and grudging acquiescence spread on his face. "Fine," he said curtly. In our family, the word *fine* was normally used to express furious deference ("I'll do it, but I'm pissed").

He signed and initialed the four-page form, and the assistant thanked him and left us alone in the room.

Jack turned to Dennis. "Dad, I just wanted to find out a little more before I signed that."

"Okay," said Dennis. "I didn't mean to be impatient. I guess I'm getting a little overwhelmed—we all are."

"I know you wanted to think about it," I offered, "but I think you did the right thing. Even if you felt rushed into it."

"Yeah, Jack," said Dennis. "You heard Dr. Friedman talking to us earlier about how far they've come in treating what you have. Letting them use whatever they can to help others—"

"I know, Dad. I just wanted to decide for myself."

The friction between father and son hung in the air. Then Dennis spoke. "I'm glad you signed it. I'm sorry, though—I didn't mean to be bossy or to get annoyed."

Jack's face softened a little. "It's okay."

The door opened and someone led us to another waiting area, this one smaller and with turquoise chairs. Soon a fifty-something nurse called us into another exam room and began to outline what would happen during the next twenty-four hours. She asked Jack all about himself and his medical history, then explained what to expect throughout the day.

"Now, are you getting hungry for lunch?" she asked him.

"Yeah."

"Good," she said. "One very important thing you need to do today is to eat lunch. When we're done here, you'll go back out to the first waiting room and finish up with someone who goes over insurance. You'll be admitted to the hospital after that, this afternoon. But before you check in at Admissions, I'd like you to go out and get a big lunch somewhere. Okay?"

Jack offered a smile. "Okay." He glanced at Dennis.

"Go wherever you like," said the nurse. "Go off hospital property if you want. Actually, I'd recommend it. Then, once you've eaten, come back and enter the hospital main entrance and go to the right, over to Admissions. They'll check you in, and then you'll be taken up to your room."

"Why do I have to be admitted this afternoon?"

"To get you ready for tomorrow. Don't worry–everything's going to be fine. Your mom and dad will be with you. You'll eat dinner in your room, and you'll be given some medicines to prepare you for your surgery. It's all part of the process. Now, go eat a good lunch, okay?"

"We will," said Dennis.

Back in the original waiting room, we were called into a private enclosed area on the left where an administrator questioned us and entered information in her computer. After several minutes, she instructed us to head to Hospital Admissions immediately.

"But the nurse we just saw said we could go get lunch somewhere outside the hospital first," I protested.

The administrator looked me, her eyes wide. She shook her head. "No, no, ma'am. He needs to be admitted *now*. Someone will bring a lunch tray to his room."

"Wait a minute," I said. Then I felt Dennis' hand on my shoulder.

"Okay," he said to the woman. I turned to look at him, then read his expression. He was trying to get us out of here, and had no intention of obeying her. "Are we done here, then?"

"Yes," she said. "Good luck."

We trudged out of the room and into the corridor, and Dennis put his arm around Jack. "I don't care what she said," he whispered. "We're going out to lunch."

Jack managed a laugh. "Way to go, Dad."

"We heard that nurse earlier," said Dennis. "We're going to do what *she* told us, not what that lady said."

I gave Dennis a look. "But–"

"No sense arguing with her, Jule–she wasn't going to change her mind, no matter what the nurse said. We're getting out of here right now to go have lunch somewhere. What do you feel like eating, Jack?"

Twenty minutes later, we sat down at a table in a Firehouse Subs around the corner from the hospital. It was a relief to be in a normal atmosphere, even if only for a while.

The three of us chatted as we ate our subs and laughed about how Dennis had led the administrator to believe we would obey her directions.

"There was no way I was going to let her keep us from going out to lunch," Dennis said to Jack. "But she wasn't going to back down."

Jack shook his head. "Nope, she wasn't. I'm glad you just said okay and then we got away from her."

I smiled. "I was ready to argue with her."

"Wouldn't have worked," said Dennis. "Would have been a waste of time. Anyway, how do you feel now, after this morning's appointment, Jack?"

"Better."

"He said we won't know what type of tumor it is until next week, right?" said Dennis.

"That's what I understood," I said. "If it's a germinoma, that's probably good."

"Why?" asked Jack.

"I read about it online. It sounded like it's one of the most curable kinds. It's the same kind Lance Armstrong had–"

Jack jumped back in his seat. "What? Are you saying–"

"Relax," I said. "I'm just saying what *kind*, not *where*. His was in his testes, but yours is in your brain. Same kind, but different locations."

Jack blew out a breath. "Okay."

"I read that, too," said Dennis. "Mom's right. And Lance is doing fine."

Jack shook his head. "As long as no one messes with little Jack, or either of his two buddies–"

We burst out laughing. "They won't," said Dennis. "Trust me."

* * *

We pulled into the circular drive in front of Duke Hospital, and Jack and I got out of the car. Dennis left to go park in another parking deck, this one across the street. Jack and I walked into the building and followed the signs to Admissions on the right side of a large atrium. Doctors, nurses, and other hospital workers scurried by, their shoes squeaking on the tan checkered floor. Boxy armchairs the color of tangerines sat among huge potted green plants and in between thick columns made of faux stone in a neutral hue. Huge rectangles of florescent lights bore down on us. Over to our left was an enclosed courtyard topped by a glass spiky dome, its large geometric panes outlined in black.

Thin, raised capital letters the same off-white color as the wall spelled *Admissions* on an eyebrow-like piece of concrete. Underneath it, a worker sat at a desk, entering information in a computer. Next to her, another worker was installed behind a check-in counter.

I braced myself emotionally. Once Jack was admitted to the hospital, the last hint of normalcy would disappear. I'd been suppressing my fears about what would happen to him for weeks, and now that he was about to be admitted, they crashed to the surface. I trembled.

What if he went into a coma? What if he had to learn to walk or talk again? What if he lost his sight? What if the part of brain that controlled emotions didn't work anymore?

What if he died?

Whatever happened, life before Duke was over, and life after it was a question at best. I could keep assuring myself—and Jack—that everything would work out, but I didn't know that to be true. I couldn't protect him any longer. His fate was out of my control.

We walked over to the check-in counter and Jack gave his name. Someone whose job it was to be here day after day, who never had to go where we were going, handed him a clipboard with several forms to fill out. We found two chairs next to each other in front of a noisy wide fountain.

"Mom? Would you fill these out for me?"

I took the clipboard. "Sure. I'll ask you anything I don't know. When I'm done, you can sign them."

"Thanks."

I was still writing when Dennis arrived. When I finished, Jack added his signature, and we walked back to the counter and handed them over.

"Thank you," said the worker. "Have a seat and wait until you hear your name."

Almost an hour later, the three of us were escorted to the room assigned to Jack. A nurse came in, introduced herself, and said that after tomorrow's surgery, he would be moved to a different, larger room. "Since it's going to change, I wouldn't give this room number to anyone who might try to call you through the hospital's main desk," she said. "Wait until tomorrow, and give out that room number."

She explained what she would be doing tonight to get Jack ready for surgery. In a little while he would get an IV and some medication that would prepare his brain for the operation. He wouldn't feel much effect, and should be able to sleep tonight.

Then she gave Dennis and me an apologetic smile. "I'm sorry, but only one of you can stay with him overnight. When he's moved over to his new room, both of you can."

Dennis glanced at me, then at Jack.

"Who wants to stay?" asked the nurse. She turned to Jack. "Who do you want to stay with you tonight?"

"Mom," said Jack. "Do you mind, Dad? Is that okay?"

"Sure. That's fine." He put his hand on Jack's arm.

"You can stay until about nine o'clock," the nurse said to Dennis. "Are you staying in a hotel?"

"Yes. What time can I come back in the morning?"

"Early," she said. "They'll come in and get him about six o'clock. You can come in around five-thirty."

"Good," said Dennis. "I'll be here at five-thirty on the dot."

The nurse left, and Dennis and I sat down on chairs next to the bed. Jack was still in his street clothes, but I knew he'd have to change into a hospital gown soon, and the IV would follow. He turned on the television and searched for a sports channel.

"Julie, I could go to the hotel now and pick up whatever you need to stay overnight," Dennis said.

"That would be great. Thanks." I made a list on a scrap of paper.

"I'll be back as soon as I can," he said. "See you soon."

Jack and I watched TV until the nurse reappeared with a hospital gown. "I got the longest one I could find," she said. "The opening goes in the back. You can keep your underwear on if you like."

Jack gave her a look, then took the gown. She walked out.

"I'll go to the hall while you change," I said. I stepped outside the door and reentered when Jack called.

We passed the time not saying much and watching television. Before long, a different nurse came in and inserted the IV. I was glad the process of getting Jack ready was on track, but it hurt to watch the big needle going into his arm. He took it in stride, though.

Soon, Dennis came in carrying a small bag. "Thanks, honey," I said.

"No problem." He glanced at the IV. "How's everything going, Jack?"

"Fine."

"They should bring in his dinner soon," I offered.

"Good," said Dennis. "When they do, I'll go down to the cafeteria and get us a couple of sandwiches, Jule."

Forty minutes later, all three of us were eating dinner. The TV was still on, providing a distraction and background noise. Later, someone picked up Jack's tray, and just before nine, the original nurse came in.

"I'm sorry," she said to Dennis. "It's time to go."

He stood reluctantly. "Okay." With a gentle smile, he leaned toward Jack and grabbed his hand. "See you in the morning, okay?"

"Okay, Dad."

"Sleep well, Jack. I love you."

"Love you, too, Dad."

I followed Dennis outside to the hall to say goodnight. We closed the door, and then I burst into tears.

"Oh, Dennis. I'm so scared!" I whispered.

He put his arms around me and pulled me close. "I know. I am, too."

We stood there holding each other for a minute. "Want to say a quick prayer together?" he asked.

I nodded and with much effort, stifled my sobs. We separated but stood close, facing each other, our hands clasped.

He spoke the words on both our hearts. "Father, please protect Jack, and let the surgery tomorrow go well. Please let the doctors heal him. Let him live."

My tears returned as he spoke, and we said an Our Father together and then opened our eyes.

"Here," said Dennis, giving me a handkerchief. "You can't go back in there and let him see you like this."

"I know." I wiped my face, then took a deep breath. With effort, I composed myself. "Better?"

"A little," said Dennis, tears filling his own eyes. "God, we're both basket cases."

A nurse passed by, offering a sympathetic glance.

"Come on, Julie," said Dennis. "Courage."

I smiled weakly and kissed him. "I'm all right now."

"Sure?"

"Yeah. See you early in the morning."

"Okay. I love you."

"I love you, too." He turned to leave, and I walked back into Jack's room wearing my bravest face.

Chapter 9

June 29 - 30

We could never learn to be brave and patient
if there were only joys in the world.

— Helen Keller

"You okay, Mom?"

"Yeah. No problem." I walked to the other side of the bed and sat down.

"Dad didn't mind that I picked you to stay tonight, did he?"

"No. It's just for tonight, anyway. We'll both be with you the whole rest of the time."

"I know."

Our nurse came back in, bringing some paperwork with her. She looked at Jack. "Doing okay?"

He nodded. "I guess."

"Anything you want to ask me?" she said, marking on a form.

He paused. "No."

She glanced at me, then looked back at the patient. "Well, I have a question for you."

"Okay," said Jack.

"Your chart says you're a Roman Catholic. Is that correct?"

"Yep."

"Okay. Would you like to meet with a priest tonight?"

Jack sucked in a breath, and I waited. "No, thank you."

"Okay."

"Are you sure?" I asked gently.

He looked right at me. "Yes."

"Do you want to think about it?" I persisted.

"No, Mom. I'm sure."

"That's fine," said the nurse. "I just wanted to ask. Mrs. McDermott, you'll find a pillow, some sheets and a blanket in the cabinet."

"Thank you."

She picked up her paperwork, said she'd be back to check on him later, and left.

I reached for Jack's arm. "Just let me know if you change your mind, all right?"

"Okay, Mom, but I'm not going to. I don't want to meet with some priest I don't even know, and I don't want to make a confession or do anything like that."

"Okay, fine. It's your decision."

"Besides, I'm not going to die."

"She wasn't saying—"

"I know she wasn't, but that's why people see priests in hospitals."

"But—"

"Really, Mom. I just don't want to see a priest."

"Okay." It *was* his decision. But I wondered if I would later regret not pushing him.

We watched TV again in silence. After about an hour, Jack turned to me. "I'm getting tired. I should probably try to go to sleep."

"Okay. I'm going to the bathroom to change into my pajamas." I emerged a few minutes later, grabbed the bedding, and spread the sheet on the sofa.

"Mom?"

"Yeah, babe?"

"I'm getting scared again. I feel like I did last night, but worse."

I walked over to him and took his hand. "It's going to be okay."

"How do you know, though?"

"I don't know, but I have faith. I believe Dr. Friedman is the right doctor, and everything's going to go fine."

"What if it doesn't?"

"Here's the thing. When he explained everything to us this morning–"

"I know, Mom, and I know I agreed to have the surgery. But now–I mean, in a few hours, he's going to operate on my brain! He's going to cut out part of my skull!" His eyes were wild. "What if something goes wrong? What if I die?"

"You won't! Nothing is going to go wrong."

"Mom–"

"Look. I know this is terrifying. Frankly, I'm terrified, too, but we have to have courage about this. As far as him cutting out your skull and putting it back, and what he does to remove the tumor, well, we just can't go there. Let's not even imagine it. Let's just let the doctor do what he's trained to do, what he does very well, and let's not picture *any* of it."

He put his hand over his forehead and eyes.

I continued, "Let's just think about how you're going to go to sleep, and when you wake up, it will be all over and the tumor will be gone. Okay?"

Tears began to flow down Jack's face. "Oh my God, Mom. I'm so afraid."

"I know, baby." I put my arms around him and gave him a hug. "Being brave doesn't mean you don't have fear. We'll get through this, I promise."

He took a deep breath and exhaled. "I love you, Mom."

"I love you, too."

* * *

Somehow, we both fell asleep. I heard Jack rustle once or twice during the night, but he didn't wake, even when a nurse came in to check on his IV. Then, before I thought it was time to get up, the door opened and a sliver of light pierced the room like a dagger.

"Julie?" whispered Dennis. "Are you awake?"

I sat up, nodded, and went over to hug him.

"It's five-thirty," he said.

I dressed, brushed my teeth and put my contacts in. No need for makeup today. I walked back into the dark room and sat on the sofa next to Dennis.

"How did your night go?"

"Okay. But we talked before we went to sleep. He's so frightened."

He nodded. "I guess we all are."

We sat waiting, and in no time, a new nurse opened the door and spoke quietly. "It's almost time."

Dennis stood and walked over to Jack, who hadn't roused from his slumber. I went to stand next to him as the nurse checked his IV. Then he woke with a start.

"What's happening?"

"It's all right, Jack," said Dennis. "The nurse is here. Mom and I are with you."

He rubbed his eyes. "Okay."

"You might want to use the bathroom," said the nurse.

He got up and lumbered over. The nurse rolled the IV pole behind him, standing outside the closed bathroom door. A few minutes later, he was back in bed.

"Now," she said, "they'll be in to get you soon. Your parents can walk alongside of you. They'll take you down to pre-op and someone will go over everything with you. The doctor will come in and talk to all of you before surgery."

"Thank you," I said.

Minutes later, two orderlies came in with a rolling gurney. Fully awake now, Jack slid onto it. Then we all began the short journey to the operating room.

I moved on automatic through the neutral corridor. It was very quiet at this hour, when most people were still asleep or just getting up for the start of an ordinary day.

But this particular day, June 30, 2010, would be the least normal day of our lives.

One of the orderlies pressed a round, silver flat button on the wall, and brown double doors buzzed open into a large room divided by pale green curtains hanging from the ceiling. We walked alongside Jack past several closed partitions and took an abrupt right into an empty space. They rolled him in and positioned him facing out; Dennis and I hovered on either side. Then they pulled the curtain around on its metal rings to define our area, and bid us goodbye.

Jack's IV bag was over to his right, and a machine anchored on the wall behind it beeped and buzzed.

"Oh, God," said Jack, turning to look. "It's just like in our skit. 'Drip, drip, buzz!'"

Dennis' eyes met mine, then traveled to Jack. "Pretty realistic, huh?"

The three of us waited, silence stretching out between us like a high tension wire. Then a short, blonde forty-something nurse opened our curtain and popped in.

"Hi, everybody," she said. "I'm Debbie. I'll be your nurse in pre-op."

"Hello," said Dennis.

"Now," she said with a business-like air, "tell me where the tumor is."

I gave Dennis a look. Did she—or did the doctors—not know? Or was it routine to ask the patient?

"It's behind his eyes," said Dennis. "In the middle."

"They have his MRI," I began.

"Okay, ma'am. Don't worry. I just don't have that information. That's why I'm asking *you*."

"You don't?" asked Dennis. He glanced at me. "Why not?"

"It's okay, I promise," she said. "I just need to know if it's midline, or if the incision will be some other place."

"We met with Dr. Friedman yesterday," I said. "He explained everything, but I don't know exactly."

Jack was propped on his elbows now, alarm spreading on his face. "Ask the doctor," he said.

Debbie gave him a scolding look, then raised her voice. "I repeat, is it midline, or not?"

Just then the curtain parted, and another nurse in pastel blue scrubs appeared. "Debbie, come with me, please," she said sternly. "You're needed elsewhere."

Debbie whirled toward her. "What?"

"Just come, please."

They both disappeared, and the three of us relaxed.

"*That* was weird," said Jack.

I looked at Dennis, but held my tongue. I could tell he was as disturbed as I was about what had just transpired.

"Yeah," he said. "She's gone, though. Let's not worry about it."

"But I agree with Jack—"

"In any case," interrupted Dennis, "let's wait for Dr. Friedman. They said he would come see us. Obviously, Debbie didn't know what was going on, but when the doctor comes in, we can talk to him."

I turned to Jack. "Dad's right." I suspected that Dennis wanted to keep him from freaking out any further. Truth told, we were all tightly wound at the moment, and if we talked about Debbie any more, it might push us over the edge.

Just then, Dr. Friedman opened the curtain and pulled it shut behind him. He looked tired, maybe because it was so early. "Good morning, folks." He walked up to Jack. "How are you doing?"

"Okay," said Jack. "That nurse that was just in here didn't seem to know what was going on, though. She asked us where the incision was going to be."

Dr. Friedman shook his head slightly. "Don't worry about her. She won't be back."

"Good," said Jack. "She made me kind of nervous."

Dr. Friedman touched Jack's arm. "Everything's going to be fine. A new nurse will be in soon, and she knows exactly what's going on. The anesthesiologist will be in as well, and will have some more forms for you to sign."

"Thank you, Doctor," said Dennis.

He looked at Dennis, then at me. "Of course. Now, how are the two of you?"

"Okay," I said. "Now that you're here."

He smiled. "If you have any questions, go ahead and ask me now. You won't see me again until after surgery."

Dennis and I exchanged glances. I shook my head.

"I don't think we do, Doctor," he said. "Do you, Jack?"

"No, I guess not."

"All right," said Dr. Friedman. "Sounds good. See you later."

He left, and a different nurse appeared. "I'm Rachel," she said. "You saw the doctor?"

"Yeah," said Jack.

"Good. Everything's on track. Dr. Friedman just finished with another patient who came in as an emergency surgery. Not to worry, though. Everything is going forth as planned."

Dennis threw me a concerned look, his eyes wide. He turned back to Rachel. "Is that–normal? I mean–"

"Yes, it's fine," she said. "It happens. Dr. Friedman can handle anything. Your next visitor will be the anesthesiologist." She popped out.

Before we had time to discuss this news, a tall fifty-something gray-haired man in green scrubs opened the curtain and walked over to Jack's side.

"Hello, everybody," he said, looking around. "I'm Dr. Warner. I'll be in charge of Jack's anesthesiology team."

"Good morning," said Dennis.

"Hello," I said.

"How are you, Jack?" said the doctor.

"I'm hanging in there."

"Good. There are some things I need to go over with you, and then I have a couple more forms for you to sign."

"Okay."

Dr. Warner's voice was soft and reassuring. He explained what his team would do to monitor Jack from the moment he arrived in the operating room until he woke up hours later in Recovery. "We'll take good care of you."

"What if I wake up during it?"

Dr. Warner raised his eyebrows. "That's very rare, but–"

"It can happen, though, right?"

"Well, yes, but the chance of it is tiny. Miniscule."

I was stunned that Jack feared waking during surgery; the possibility hadn't even crossed my mind. Then I thought of our conversation of last night when I had urged him not to picture what would happen once he was put to sleep. Maybe even the remote chance of waking up while his brain was being operated on was more than he could handle.

"Now," Dr. Warner said to me and Dennis. "How are you two?"

"Okay, so far," said Dennis. "We know he's in good hands."

"We do our very best," said the anesthesiologist. He smiled. "It won't be long before he's up and around, and you all are on your way back home to Atlanta. Duke is a wonderful place, but if you're like most of our patients, you'll say that your favorite memory of it is the way it looks in your rearview mirror."

Dennis offered a weak smile. "I'm sure we'll be glad to see that."

The doctor turned back to Jack. "There's one more thing I need to explain. After we put you to sleep, a catheter will be inserted into your body. When you wake up, it will still be there. It will be removed later."

"What's a catheter?"

I braced myself. Surely he knew what it was. But if he didn't—

"It's a tube that continually drains your urine, to keep you from having to go to the bathroom."

A concerned look spread on Jack's face. "Exactly *where* is it inserted?"

"In your penis—"

In a split second, Jack raised himself to a sitting position, his body tense and on alert. He looked as if he were about to jump out of his skin. "*What?*"

Reflexively, we put our hands on Jack's shoulders and Dr. Warner put his on Jack's arm. Dennis and I stifled chuckles, and I cupped my hand over my mouth. Evidently, what he'd just been told was just as frightening as having his skull drilled into or his brain operated on.

The anesthesiologist cleared his throat. "Don't worry about it. A lot of guys react the same way, but I promise, you won't feel a thing."

"What about when it comes out?" asked Jack.

"It won't hurt."

"I've heard *that* before, and it wasn't true."

"It'll be fine."

"But—can't we skip this?" Jack pleaded. "I *know* I can hold it—"

He was slightly on the naïve side, and his entreaty reminded me of his proposal back in May that he wear "really strong glasses" in hopes of avoiding surgery then. The mama bear in me wanted once again to protect him from fear and from any level of discomfort, but she couldn't—again.

"I'm sorry," said Dr. Warner. "The surgery's going to take several hours, so we can't skip it. It's routine."

Jack lay back down and heaved a sigh. "Dad—"

"Don't worry," said Dennis. "They'll take care of you. Everything's going to be all right."

"Your dad's right. Now, I have a few more forms for you to sign, and then we're good to go." He produced a clipboard and pen.

"I thought I signed everything already."

"Almost," said the anesthesiologist. "This is a consent form for me, and an authorization to bill insurance. This last one is a called an advance directive. Basically, it's a document that tells us what your wishes are, if you can't be resuscitated."

"You mean, like, a will? A makeshift will?"

Dr. Warner paused for a second. "Not really a will, like you might think. It's just about your health and your body, not any possessions you have. It instructs us, for example, not to take extraordinary measures, if you become brain dead."

Jack clutched my hand with his left one. "You mean—"

The doctor took a reassuring tone. "It's also routine for surgeries like the one you're about to have. It's just a formality. It's rarely, if ever, needed. Trust me."

Jack looked over it, signed, and Dr. Warner bid all of us goodbye.

"Mom, Dad. Oh, my God," said Jack.

"Don't worry," said Dennis. "We'll see you when you wake up. We love you, Jack."

Before I had a chance to speak, two hospital workers came in to take him to the operating room, positioning themselves on either side of the gurney. This was it.

Jack squeezed my hand. "Mom! Mom!"

Tears streamed down my face. "It's okay, baby. I love you." I leaned down and kissed his forehead.

Would this be the last time he would talk to me? Would it be the last time I would ever see him? What was going to happen?

Was he going to live?

Dennis offered him a final word of assurance as the workers rolled him away, and in a flash, he was gone.

Chapter 10

June 30

"Live through it," Call said. "That's all we can do."

— Larry McMurtry, *Lonesome Dove*

A nurse led Dennis and me through a set of double doors into a huge, rectangular waiting room, and over to a check-in desk at one end of the room. The woman sitting behind the desk greeted us and handed me a round black pager.

"Have a seat and make yourselves comfortable," she said. "When this lights up and vibrates, come back and I'll give you an update."

"Thank you," I said, taking Dennis' hand.

"There's coffee and some vending machines over on the left," she added, motioning toward a nearby group of seats where people sat watching television.

"Thanks," said Dennis. We turned and headed away to find a place to sit.

The room was divided into small waiting areas by clouded glass panels, each seating group half populated by families of other neurosurgery patients. Every area contained U-shaped rows of identical gray and tan cloth and vinyl chairs with blond wood armrests. Worn neutral carpeting muted our steps as we traipsed to the far end of the room, away from other people.

Wordlessly, we plopped down into two chairs facing the direction we had come, and I dropped my purse on the floor. Windows lined the wall on our right; on our left was a tiled wide corridor next to a wood paneled wall. A wood bar at waist level was bolted to the wall and ran the length of it. The room smelled of a mixture of burned coffee and Pledge, with a hint of antiseptic.

I stared into space, feeling numb and disoriented. My life had been on hold ever since Jack's birthday—I'd felt as if time itself had been suspended. Nothing else mattered besides getting him well. We'd been preparing for this day for weeks, and I'd known that it was coming. But now that it was happening, I wondered how we got here.

Despite my effort not to, I imagined Jack's long body stretched out as the anesthesiology team worked on him. How much time had he been awake after he'd been taken away? How frightened was he? Had he cried? Had anyone offered him comforting words?

During the surgery, he would be lying on his front with his head clamped in something like a vise, his long arms carefully positioned and secured. I supposed that Dr. Friedman would make the incision, and cut into his skull. A vision flashed in my head of a hapless French monarch under the guillotine.

I shuddered, pushed the image away, and pulled my Kindle out of my bag; Dennis had brought his book and had opened it. We would be in this room for the better part of the day, and I had to think of something other than what was happening to Jack at any moment. The nurse had advised us that his surgery would take at least four hours, and wouldn't begin for at least an hour from now; our pager would light up when it did.

I stared at the latest nonfiction book I had downloaded, a combination business and psychology tome whose title escapes me now. Unable to process the words, I turned right and gazed out the window.

I heard a small commotion and saw a group of Hispanic women approach our semicircle and fill the empty seats. For a second, I was annoyed that they had invaded our space. Then they all produced rosary beads, and began quietly saying the rosary together in Spanish.

I wasn't a rosary-praying sort of person, and although Dennis had been raised a Catholic, he wasn't that sort, either. With one son in the seminary, you'd think we would be, but—except for a rare rosary service at church—it just wasn't us. However, listening to the group of women comforted me somewhat, and my irritation at their intrusion melted away. If God could hear them praying—and I felt sure that he could—then he could hear our prayers, whether we spoke them out loud or not.

Dear Lord, let Jack live.

Maybe if I prayed that over and over, like the women prayed the rosary, God would hear me. I kept praying silently, pleading with God to let Jack not only live, but be healed. To be completely rid of his brain tumor. To not have cancer. To not need to learn to walk or talk again. To be the Jack I knew, able to do anything. To be 100 percent healthy.

Was it too much to ask?

I prayed for Jack's tumor to be the "good" kind—a germinoma—the kind with the best rate of cure. I prayed that he would be able to get through whatever other treatment might lie ahead—chemotherapy, radiation, or both. I prayed that he would make it.

I asked God to guide the surgeon's hand.

I kept my eyes closed, but I didn't cry. After several minutes, I opened them and tried to read. This time, I was able to. Perhaps if I just acted like everything was all right, it would be. If I trusted in the doctors, and in God, Jack would live, and he would be all right.

Please, God.

* * *

The pager lit up and vibrated, its red lights flashing. I jumped up. Dennis looked up at me. "I suppose that means it's started," he said.

"I'm going to find out."

"Okay."

In less than thirty seconds, I stood in front of the desk and presented the pager to the woman.

She took it and silenced it. "The surgery has begun." She gave it back to me. "Someone will come and let me know how things are going after an hour or two, and then it will light up again. When it does, come back and I'll update you."

"Thank you," I said. I turned, trudged back to my seat, and repeated what the woman had told me.

Dennis put his arm around me and pulled me toward him. "I've been praying for him."

I looked into his eyes. "So have I." A lump formed in my throat, and fresh tears fell down my cheeks. "Oh, Dennis."

"I know. We just have to keep on praying. Have you let everyone back at home know what's going on?"

"I emailed Mom and Dad, and sent a message to my Bible study group."

"Good." He had called his mom the day before and she had told the family. Jack had said it was okay now to tell everybody, but he'd repeated his request that they not post anything on Facebook.

I grabbed my phone, a BlackBerry, out of my purse and checked my email. "I have messages from the Bible study."

Almost everyone in the group had sent emails saying they were thinking about us and praying for us. I read each one over and over. "Look," I said, handing Dennis the phone.

He read them and gave the phone back to me. "I'm glad. How are you doing, Jule?"

"Okay. How about you?"

"The same."

One of the Hispanic women stood, holding her blinking pager, and walked to the desk. A moment later, she was back, talking to her group. All the women got up and followed her toward the desk and then past it, turning a corner.

Their loved one's surgery was over.

Watching them go, I felt a pang of jealousy. They had gotten here after us, yet they were already leaving. They were going to see their loved one, whom I assumed was going to be all right. Of course, I wanted everyone in the waiting room to receive good news. But our loved one was still on the table. We wouldn't find out if he was okay for some time. We had to stay here, keep waiting, and keep praying.

For the next three hours, other people came and went; those who'd arrived before us left. Our pager lit up a couple more times, and we were advised that everything was going fine. For short periods, we read our books, taking occasional breaks to go to the restroom or get water. Though I hadn't eaten, I wasn't hungry. Dennis got a granola bar from the vending machine.

I couldn't pray nonstop, but frequently, I stopped reading and said another prayer. Then a female hospital worker appeared from around the corner, rolling a cart down the tiled corridor on our left. She stopped abruptly, unloaded a box from the top of the cart, and began setting something up. I wondered what it could be.

It was a harp. She set a stool beside it, sat down, and started playing, filling the room with music.

Dennis and I exchanged looks, and all of a sudden, I broke into sobs.

"What is it, Julie? Are you okay?"

I shook my head. "I was–but now I'm not. That music–it's making me freak out! It's like it's God, or Saint Peter, welcoming Jack into heaven!"

He pulled me to him. "Oh, babe. No. Jack hasn't died."

"I know I'm being irrational. It's just that I was fine until that lady got here and started playing! I can't stand it–I'm going to the restroom again." I stood, picked up my bag, and hurried away.

I stayed in the ladies' room for a good fifteen minutes, getting a hold of myself and splashing water on my face. I found a tube of lipstick and applied it. I took a deep breath and walked back over to Dennis. The damn harp lady was still playing, and my heart was in my throat.

I had left our pager with him, and now it lit up again. "I'll go," I said. I took it and made my way to the desk.

"The surgery is over," said the woman. "You can leave the pager here, then gather the rest of your family members. The doctor will meet you here in a few minutes and take you down that hall past the elevators to a consultation room." She motioned to her right.

"Thank you." I hurried back to Dennis and told him.

Five minutes later, Dr. Friedman appeared and walked up to us. "Hello, folks," he said. "Follow me."

He led us down the hall and opened a door under a blue and white sign that read "Consultation." We entered the small, stark room and sat down on the same kind of chairs as the ones in the surgery waiting room. He closed the door. A box of tissues sat on a small table in the middle of the featureless room.

"Jack's doing well," he said. "It took a long time—longer than I thought it would. But he did fine. In fact, he may be doing better than I am right now." He did look exhausted. His eyes were glassy and red. "He'll be in Recovery for a while, and then he'll be moved over to ICU. You'll be able to see him then. He'll be with a nurse there who will monitor him constantly."

"So, the surgery—" began Dennis.

"I got most of the tumor out," said Dr. Friedman. "Not quite all. But remember, I said I may not be able to. It was a tough one, and difficult to remove. It was spidery, and very close to his optic nerves and pituitary gland."

I was both relieved and worried. What did this mean?

"That's okay, though," continued Dr. Friedman. "He may need radiation to target the cells I wasn't able to extract. But we can talk about that after it comes back from pathology."

We listened as he described the process and answered our questions. "I wish I could tell you now what type of tumor it is," he said, "but we just need to wait. It takes several days. It will probably be the middle of next week before we know."

"Do you know if it was malignant?" asked Dennis.

He cocked his head. "That's hard to say. It looked as if it had been growing, but I'd say that it's not *very* malignant."

"What do you mean, not 'very' malignant?" asked Dennis.

Dr. Friedman paused for a second. "I mean, in the sense of how fast it's growing, not in the sense of a stage of malignancy. The tumor isn't benign—it is malignant. But we know it hadn't spread to his spine—the MRIs showed that. However, it had probably been growing over time. Since the brain sits inside the skull, eventually, an expanding tumor has nowhere to go—it creates pressure, which results in all kinds of problems, like the vision problems he had."

"Will his shunt stay in?" I asked. "Or did it come out?"

"Oh, it's still there," said the doctor. "And it needs to stay there. There's no reason to take it out."

"But–" I started.

"It's fine, really," he said. "It won't cause him any problems. Taking it out would pose an unnecessary risk."

"Thank you, Doctor," said Dennis.

"Now, unless you have any more questions, I'm going to go and rest. You'll see me again over the next few days and we'll talk some more. Right now, you should go and get out of here for a couple of hours. Go get a Coke or a coffee somewhere away from the hospital, or go have an early dinner. Come back around six-thirty. Tell them your son had neurosurgery, and someone will take you down to him. You'll be able to be at his side this evening, but you can't stay overnight. You can come back early tomorrow, though. By then, he should be moved into a patient room."

I felt numb. Jack was alive, and most of–*most of*–his brain tumor had been removed. But the doctor said it wasn't benign. Was he truly okay? How was he going to heal from this surgery? What else would he have to do? What kind of tumor was it?

What was his future?

* * *

We took the elevator down and walked out the hospital main entrance, then across the street to the parking garage.

"What do you want to do?" asked Dennis.

"I don't know. Maybe go to the hotel and take a shower."

"Okay. After that, why don't we go get dinner, like he suggested, and then go back?"

"All right. I'm getting hungry, anyway."

"Me too."

Back in the room, Dennis called his mom and gave her a report. I got dressed, called my parents and did the same. Everyone was relieved the surgery was over, and asked how Jack was doing. I sent messages to my Bible study group and other close friends to let them know.

We went to the same restaurant we had been to on Monday night with Jack and ordered right away. The place wasn't crowded—it was too early. We chatted nervously until our food arrived and after we ate, we headed back to the hospital parking deck. In the hospital, we were escorted to the neurosurgery ICU. A nurse led us past several curtained partitions, then gently opened the last one.

"Melanie? Mr. and Mrs. McDermott are here."

A pretty, blonde nurse in her twenties turned toward us. "Hello. Come in. He's dozing on and off, but he's doing fine."

Jack was sprawled on a hospital bed, his eyes closed and his shoulders and head propped up by pillows and a raised mattress. A huge, thick white bandage was wrapped around his head like a turban. He looked like a soldier injured in combat. My heart rose to my throat again and tears welled in my eyes. I had known his head would be bandaged, but even so, it was hard to take. I didn't want him to see my reaction, so I took a deep breath and composed myself. He needed me to be strong.

He stirred slightly and opened his eyes. "Mom? Dad?"

We rushed to his left side. On his right was an IV stand and bag—various tubes ran from somewhere on his body to it.

"Hi, sweetie," I said, taking his hand.

"Hey, Jack," said Dennis. "We're here. It's all over."

"You playin' me, Dad?" he mumbled.

Dennis shook his head and smiled. "No, no, I'm not playin' you. It's over. You're all done, and we're with you now."

"Oh, thank God," Jack breathed.

"Hey, Jack," said the nurse. "I'm Melanie. I'll be taking care of you, and your dad is right. You're all done. I'll be asking you some questions from time to time, but in between, you can rest."

"Okay. I'm just really tired."

"I know," said Melanie. "I'll let you sleep as much as I can. But I have to wake you every fifteen minutes."

I turned to her. "Every fifteen minutes? Why?"

"I need to monitor him neurologically. Don't worry—it's routine. He'll still be able to rest. Then later on, after you leave, he's going to have a post-op MRI."

"Tonight?" asked Dennis.

She nodded. "After that, he'll come back here, and someone will be with him all through the night. He won't be alone. When you come back in the morning, he'll be assigned to a patient room. You can stay with him there until he's released."

The thought of Jack having another MRI—after what he had been through today—upset me. Couldn't it wait? If not, there had to be a medical reason. So I pushed the vision of him sliding into the MRI machine from my mind. This was Duke Hospital, and these people knew what they were doing. I just hoped they would be gentle with him.

"Jack?" said Melanie. "Don't fall asleep yet. I need to ask you some questions."

"Okay," he mumbled.

"Who's the president?"

"Obama."

"Good! What year is it?"

"2010."

"Okay. Now, I need to you hold out your arms, the way you would if you were holding a pizza box."

He did as requested.

"Now grab my arms and pull on them."

He did.

"Great! You can drop them now."

"Can I go to sleep?"

"Not yet. I have just a few more questions."

Jack sighed.

"What's your birthday?"

"May 8."

"Where do you go to college?"

"University of Georgia."

After a few more questions, Melanie let him sleep. I stayed next to him, watching him and offering silent prayers of thanksgiving. A quarter of an hour later, she woke him and queried him again, varying the questions. All seemed designed to test his memory and gross motor skills. I wondered what else he would be tested on, and when. Though I understood why the nurse couldn't let him sleep, I wished she could.

After a few periods of questioning, however, he got more wakeful, not less. Soon he was joking with Melanie, and he seemed to have noticed how attractive she was. He offered weak smiles and did the best he could to flirt with her, even telling her a Tiger Woods joke. I was only a little surprised, and very relieved. He was himself. He could think, he could talk, and he could be funny.

His brain was working.

However, he was wounded. I worried about what it looked like under his bandage and whether the titanium screws were doing their job. I worried about his *skull*. I forced myself not to think about his brain itself, or what it had just been through. My mind raced with thoughts about what his future would be—both immediate and long-term.

I wanted to make him all better now, but I had to trust others to do it. I didn't want to leave him that night, but around nine o'clock, Melanie said we had to go.

"We'll take good care of him, I promise," she said. "He'll have the MRI in an hour or two, but don't worry. He'll come back here afterward and we'll watch him all night long."

Dennis and I reluctantly said goodbye and kissed our precious son goodnight, then made our way out to the car and the hotel.

Chapter 11

July 1 - 3

Whether you think you can, or think you can't,
you're right.

– Henry Ford

Early the next morning, we were all together in Jack's new patient room.

His bandage had been changed, and we were told that he had gotten through last night's MRI just fine. When he felt like it, he could eat. His vitals were being checked at regular intervals, and his blood sugar was being monitored.

We hadn't seen Dr. Friedman yet, but another doctor who was on the team came in and introduced himself. He asked Jack a few questions, then said a physical therapist would be in soon to help him get out of bed and start moving around.

"Should he get up yet?" I asked. "Can't he rest?"

The doctor regarded me for a moment. "He can rest for now, but he needs to get up this morning, and begin to get better. That means pushing himself up to a sitting position, standing and walking, even if he feels weak."

"But—"

He held up a hand. "I know that, as his mother, you're going to want to help him. But you have to stop yourself, or you'll delay his recovery. Let us do our job, okay, Mom?"

"Okay," I said uneasily. They could do what they needed to do, and I would cooperate. However, I would be watching, and I wasn't going anywhere.

Jack looked at me. "Mom. I'll be fine."

Once the doctor left, Dennis quietly reiterated his message. "Jule, I know it's going to be hard, but we have to trust them. Okay?"

I nodded. I hadn't slept well, thinking about my boy in the hospital without me nearby. We turned on the TV and tuned it to a morning news show, keeping the volume low. After a few minutes, Jack dozed off. Half an hour later, a tall fifty-something woman with short gray hair and wearing a white pants outfit—not scrubs—opened the door.

"Good morning, Jack," she said brightly, waking him. She smiled. "My name is Mary Anne, and I'm your physical therapist. I'll be working with you today. How are you doing?"

"Fine," he said sleepily, rubbing his eyes.

"Good! Have you gotten up to go to the bathroom yet?"

"Um, no. I don't have to go."

"Okay. Well, that catheter's gone now, so you will soon. Before you do, we need to make sure you can stand up. If you need him, your dad can help you over to the toilet when you're ready."

"Okay," said Jack.

"It's good that the catheter's out," said Dennis.

171

Jack gave him a look. "That guy *lied* to me, Dad. He said it wouldn't hurt when they took it out, but it did. It hurt like *hell*." He winced.

Oh, dear. Well, that was what doctors did at times, when it came to something painful. They lied.

"Well," said Dennis, "at least it's out, and you survived."

"Let's not talk about it," said Jack.

"No, let's not," said Mary Anne. "Let's talk about getting you up and around this morning."

"When?" asked Jack.

"As soon as you can," she said. "See that chair on your right?" She motioned to an armchair snug in the corner next to the head of the bed. "Later today, I want you sitting in that, not lying down."

"But—" he began.

"Now, now. You'll get enough rest today. But you're going to get your exercise, too. And it won't hurt you to sit in the chair when you're awake."

"Fine."

"Another thing. How's your neck feel?"

"Stiff and sore."

"That's normal," said Mary Anne. "But you've got to start moving it—turning your head from side to side. No more turning your shoulders and keeping your neck straight."

"But it hurts when I try to do that."

"It's going to hurt a little, but you have to do it. If you don't, your shoulders will stiffen up too, and you won't get better—you'll hurt more. Come on, you're a big, strong guy. You can do it."

"I guess I can try."

"Good. Now, let me show you the best way to sit up and get out of bed."

Dennis and I watched while she came over to Jack's left side and helped him position his left elbow. Evidently, she wanted him to push down on it to turn his body and raise himself up, while swinging his legs to the ground. "Let me get these non-slip socks on your feet first," she said. "Goodness. What size shoe do you wear?"

"Thirteen."

"I hope these are big enough!"

She stretched them on his feet, and he cooperated, grunting as he turned and pushed on the bed to sit up. I remembered how I had felt after a caesarian section–I'd had three–and how hard it had been to get out of bed. At least he hadn't had his abdomen cut into–his core muscles should be okay. Maybe the pain in his neck was so strong that it affected them; even if not, it probably hurt a lot. But pain was mental as well as physical, and you had to fight through it.

In a few seconds, he was standing and facing me and Dennis. His hand was on Mary Anne's shoulder. "I knew you could do it!" she said. "Now, let's talk about taking a walk down the hall."

"Now? I'm a little dizzy." He took a deep breath.

"We can wait until you're ready," she said, looking up at the top of his head. "Wow. You *are* tall. Take my hand."

He did and she reached her left arm around his waist. His hospital gown reached halfway to his knees, and his long legs stuck out below it like Big Bird's. She glanced behind him.

"Ah-oh," she said. "I forgot you wouldn't be wearing any underwear right now. Dad, can you fetch a pair for him?"

Dennis hastened to grab some boxers out of the bag. "Here you go."

"Jesus," said Jack, aware now that his gown was open in the back. "I need a little privacy."

"Don't worry. We won't look," she said.

"But, my mom–"

"Oh, hush. That woman gave birth to you! She's seen your bottom before. I'm sure she wiped it a few times, too."

I turned away. "That's okay," I said. "I'll just step out into the hall for a minute."

"Thanks, Mom."

"I'm not going with her, in case you need me," said Mary Anne, "but I'll turn around while your dad helps you."

I left the room and waited right outside the cracked door, my back to it. I heard some rustling, and then Dennis called, "He's decent now."

I opened the door and entered.

Mary Anne looked up at Jack and smiled. "There, now! Ready to go for a walk?" She put her arm around his waist again.

"Fine. But don't let go of me."

"Oh, don't worry. I won't. Let me grab your IV pole. It's going with us."

The two of them shuffled around the bed and toward the corridor, and Dennis and I sat down on the small tan sofa.

"Want some coffee?" he asked me. "There's a machine down the hall."

"Sure."

Jack and Mary Anne were gone for only fifteen minutes, and when they returned, he looked exhausted. "Can I go back to bed now?" he asked her.

"How about sitting in the chair instead? You're awake, so that's where I want you."

"All day?" he asked. "I want to stretch out."

"Okay, look," she said. "Get back in bed for now. But the next time I come in, probably in less than an hour, we're going to do this little routine again, and then you're sitting in the chair. Okay?"

"Whatever you say." He sat on the bed. "See you later."

"See you soon," she said, then left.

"That wasn't so bad, was it?" I asked.

"Not really."

The door opened and a worker came in with Jack's breakfast. He placed it on the rolling tray and positioned it in front of him.

"Thanks," said Jack.

Dennis and I drank our coffee while Jack ate. Once he was finished, he dozed for a while. I checked my phone for messages. Almost everyone from my Bible study had sent another email with get well wishes and promises of continuing prayers. So had my parents, my sister, the O'Barrs, and my other close friends. I was glad to get their messages, and I wrote back, but I didn't want to talk to anyone yet. When I had spoken to my parents after the surgery, I'd had a hard time keeping it together, even though all the news had been good so far.

I looked over at Jack and watched him sleep. Here he was, less than twenty-four hours after brain surgery—a thing most people never have to face—and he'd already been up and walking around. He was getting pain medication through his IV, but I knew he must be hurting. However, he wasn't complaining about it. He wasn't cranky or upset, the way I would have been. In this battle he'd been thrown into, he had manned up. He had become a Marine.

Before long, Mary Anne returned and roused her patient. "Time to get up!"

Jack gave in to her commands with resigned but cheerful acquiescence. Their walks lasted longer and longer as the day went on. A couple of times, I accompanied them, and in between, he dutifully sat in the armchair and watched TV. By the afternoon, they were lapping the floor and even climbing the stairs to the next floor.

"He's a strong young man," Mary Anne said when they got back around three o'clock. She looked up at him. "Look at how much you've done today!"

"Yeah, yeah."

"I've enjoyed our talks, too," she said. "I like your sense of humor."

Jack smiled. "Are we done for today?"

"*We're* done, but *you're* not. I have to go, but you're going to take a few more walks this evening with your mom and dad. I'll be back tomorrow morning, bright and early!"

"Fine," said Jack, a rueful grin on his face. "See you then."

* * *

We accompanied him for two more walks around the floor. I was amazed at how well he was able to get around, less than twenty-four hours after surgery. We ate dinner in the room and then settled down to watch television. Luckily, Jack's digestive system was fine, unlike after the shunt surgery. Nurses came in at regular intervals to check on him, and continued asking him questions to test his neurological abilities. He answered everything correctly. His brain seemed to be doing fine.

I went to sleep that night with a heart full of hope and less heavy than it had been in weeks. Perhaps everything would work out. Jack was doing well so far, and that was enough for me, for the moment.

I had to keep on taking things one day at a time.

The next day, he walked with Mary Anne again and was out of bed most of the day, walking or sitting in his armchair. The doctor who had been in on Thursday came back and checked his incision. Nurses kept checking it too, and monitoring his blood sugar and vital signs. He kept working on moving his neck, which was starting to get easier. He was still on pain meds and would be for a few more days, but his appetite was strong.

Between two meals, he wanted a snack. "I want something good, though," he told us when we were alone. "Not fruit, and not another yogurt."

"One of us could go down to the cafeteria and get something for you," said Dennis. "The nurse said you could eat whatever you want now."

"That's right," I said. "I'll go downstairs and get you a snack."

"Thanks, Mom!"

Ten minutes later, I was surveying the choices in the cafeteria. I knew what Jack liked, and most of the snacks I saw weren't his type of thing. Then I spied some Krispy Kreme doughnuts, and texted Dennis to ask Jack if that's what he wanted.

The answer was an excited yes and a request for several. I put six in a bag, paid for them, and went back to the room.

"Wow," said Jack. "Real food."

Well, not really. But at least it wasn't the tasteless hospital food he had been eating so far. He devoured four doughnuts in no time. "I'll save these last two for later," he said. "Unless you guys want them?"

I shook my head.

"I don't, either," said Dennis. "Mom can put the bag in her purse."

Satiated, Jack handed me the bag and turned on a sports channel. The three of us relaxed. Twenty minutes later, a nurse came in to check on him, and got to work.

She raised her eyebrows. "Whoa. Your blood sugar has shot up considerably." She gave him a quizzical look.

Jack threw me a guilty glance and gave the nurse a sheepish look. "Oh, well, I ... Oops."

"He just ate four glazed doughnuts," Dennis admitted.

"He did?" asked the nurse. "Where did you get those?"

"Um," I said, "they said he could eat whatever he wanted, so I got them from the cafeteria." I felt like a very bad mom.

The nurse gave me and Dennis a scolding look. "Well—" she began, then turned back to Jack. "It's all right this time, but just don't OD on sweets, okay?"

"Okay," he said, lifting his eyebrows and making an I'm-sorry face.

She smiled, then left. Jack let out a deep breath. "I thought they said I *could* eat anything."

"Ah, don't worry about it," said Dennis. "You did eat four. I don't think it was that big of a deal."

"I guess we should have remembered they were still checking your blood sugar," I said.

"Wait til tomorrow before you eat the other two," said Dennis, "or until you're out of the hospital."

Early that afternoon, the doctor decided to discharge him, but emphasized that we needed to stay close to the hospital for the next several days. Soon after, Mary Anne came in for one final walking tour.

"I'm going to miss you, Jack!" she exclaimed when they got back to the room. "You take care of yourself, now, y'hear?"

"I will," Jack said, smiling. "Thanks for everything."

"No, thank *you*," she said. "You've been one of my most cooperative patients. And the one who's made me laugh the most! Good luck now."

"Thanks." Jack grinned. Once she left, he turned to his father and me. "That Mary Anne." He shook his head slightly, still smiling. "She made me work hard!"

"Which is a good thing," offered Dennis.

A nurse came in to remove his IV, gave us detailed instructions about his meds, and showed us how to clean his incision and change the dressing.

"Make sure he keeps turning his neck and keeps it loose," she said.

Dennis went to get the car and a few minutes later, an attendant showed up with a wheelchair for the trip to the hospital's main entrance. I walked alongside Jack, and when we got there, Dennis was waiting to pick us up.

Back at the hotel, we walked Jack in through the lobby and down the long hallway toward the elevator. When it opened, the three of us stepped inside, and a tall man in his thirties joined us. The door closed and the man stared at Jack's bandage.

"Ya hurt ya head?" he asked bluntly. My stomach clenched, and Dennis and I exchanged apprehensive glances.

Jack looked at the guy. "Just had brain surgery, dude."

The man's cheeks reddened. "Oh! Sorry."

"No problem," said Jack. The elevator door opened and the man scurried out. After the door closed, the three of us broke out laughing.

"Gee, buddy!" I said.

"I know!" said Jack. He made a silly face. "'*Ya hurt ya head?*'"

Dennis shrugged. "You're probably going to hear questions like that," he said as the door opened on our floor.

We walked into our hotel room and Jack sat down on one of the beds. It had been a long walk from the car. We had made a medication checklist from the discharge instructions to keep track of when he was due to take what. I pulled it out of my purse and read it over to make sure we were on schedule.

The hotel room phone rang and I picked it up.

"Mrs. McDermott? I have a delivery for your son—a Jack McDermott?"

"Yes, he's here," I said.

"I'll send it up."

"Thank you." I replaced the receiver and told Jack and Dennis. Five minutes later, a bell boy arrived with a big basket filled with two of Jack's favorite sweets: Twizzlers and Reese's Cups. The DVD "UP" was also in the basket.

"They're from Aunt Pam," said Jack, reading the card. "Wow. That was nice of her."

"Yeah, that was really nice," I said. "She'd asked me if you had seen that movie, and I told her I didn't think so."

"No, I haven't," he said. "I want to see it, though. I heard it was good."

"You can when we get home," said Dennis.

"I brought my laptop, though. I can watch it on that."

"You can?" I said. "A DVD?"

"Yep. Maybe later, we could watch it together?"

"I'd love to," I said, then made a decision. "I'm going to call Pam and thank her. You can talk to her too if you'd like."

"Sure."

Pam was glad to hear from us and happy that the basket had arrived. We didn't talk for long, but I gave her an update on Jack and asked her to tell the rest of the family. "Tell Mom and Dad I'll call them later, okay?"

"Of course," she said. "Just keep in touch, though, will you?"

"I will. We're here for several more days, and we won't know anything about the tumor until probably the middle of next week. Jack wants to talk to you now, okay?"

After they hung up, Jack said he was hungry. "That last meal I had at the hospital today wasn't that great. Can we go somewhere nearby for a bite?"

I was glad he was hungry, and that he didn't mind walking around with a huge bandage on his head. We found a Mexican restaurant in Durham called El Corral. Now that he was out of the hospital, he really could eat whatever he wanted.

When he was a little boy—and until his sophomore year in high school—he'd been a very picky eater. He never ate meat, and he ate very few vegetables. He had lived on peanut butter, eggs, milk, and carbs; "anything beige" was the family joke. Dennis and I had always been concerned about his nutrition, but our pediatrician had assured us it was fine, as long as he got enough protein.

However, extended family members had often questioned us about it. When Pam had learned of his tumor, one thing she'd asked was whether it might have been caused by eating too much peanut butter. I hadn't been able to tell if she was serious that day—but her decision to include Reece's Peanut Butter Cups in the gift basket seemed to convey an apology. Jack had discovered meat and started eating it when he began playing football, at age fifteen. Now he liked beef, chicken, most fish, and many vegetables. He was still choosy, but as long as it wasn't super spicy, Mexican food was fine.

After some tacos and tortillas, we drove over to the Duke University campus. Jack had never been there, and I wasn't sure if Dennis had. I'd only been there once or twice back when I was a student at UNC.

Dennis found a visitor parking space on a small lot near one end of campus, and we began walking toward the quad. The three of us wandered down the paved pathways between Duke's Gothic architecture. I stopped to take a couple of photos. A campus tour was taking place a short distance away. The sun shone in the sky and the temperature had risen considerably since morning. At Jack's request, we found a bench under the shade of a tree and sat down.

"I'm getting really tired again," he said.

"How do your neck and shoulders feel?" I asked, worried.

"Better than yesterday. I know we just got here, but I'd kind of like to go now, if it's okay."

"Sure," said Dennis.

"But first, maybe we could stop for ice cream somewhere?"

Dennis flashed a smile at me. "Why don't we look for a Ben and Jerry's?"

We found one over in Chapel Hill. Dennis dropped me and Jack off, then parked the car and joined us. Back at the hotel, I began to think of practical matters. "I think I'll find a Laundromat sometime tomorrow and do our laundry."

"That would be great," said Dennis. "Thanks."

"Do you guys think we could go back to Chapel Hill tomorrow?" asked Jack.

"Sure, if you feel up to it," said Dennis. "We could go there for breakfast, if you like."

After we got ready for bed, we watched TV for a while. When we turned out the lights, I listened to Jack breathing until he fell asleep. I said a silent prayer of thanksgiving that everything had gone well so far.

Then I asked God to let him get all better, to be free of cancer.

Please, Lord. Let him live.

* * *

The next morning, we drove to Chapel Hill. Jack had been here and to the UNC campus several times over the years, sometimes for football and basketball games.

"Can we go to the Carolina Coffee Shop?" he asked.

"Sounds great," said Dennis.

As Jack and all his siblings knew, I had worked at the landmark restaurant to help pay my way through college. We sat down at a wooden booth as classical music filled the air. We opened our menus, laying them on the shiny black table.

"What should we do after breakfast?" I asked.

Dennis looked at Jack. "Well, we could walk around on campus, so you can get your exercise in. It's not too far from here to the Old Well."

"Yeah, let's," said Jack. "Good idea."

"Then," continued Dennis, "maybe we could drive down to the house in Bynum where I lived one year when I was a student. You could see how far away it was, and the road I used to ride my bike on before I broke down and bought a car."

"Sure, Dad. That would be great."

Our coffee arrived and breakfast followed. In between bites, Dennis and I reminisced about our Tar Heel days. It did feel good to be in a place where we had ties and felt at home, even though it had been decades since our time here. After our visit to the Duke campus—and because of the doctors at Duke Hospital—my feelings toward our archrival had changed.

We walked through the quad, and when we got to the Old Well, the sun had risen high in the Carolina blue sky. Jack and I posed while Dennis took a photo of us. With my arm around Jack's waist, the top of my head came up to just above his shoulder. I could feel him leaning on me.

"You know that song?" I said. "'Lean On Me?'"

"Yeah, I think so," he said, smiling. All our kids had heard our sixties and seventies tunes many times over the years.

"It can be our theme song," I said, then began to sing the first few lines.

"Gosh, Mom, I love you." His eyes were watery.

I was glad my sunglasses hid mine. "I love you, too, baby."

The three of us trudged back to Franklin Street and to the car, and then Dennis drove out of town towards Pittsboro. His college house in Bynum was on the way, right on the south bank of the Haw River, several miles south of town. Of course, I'd been there with him a lot when we were young—it was where he had lived the year we started dating.

"Looks like the road it's on is closed," said Dennis as we approached. "I think we can get there another way, though. I'm going to turn around and go back."

He found another street we could turn onto. The house was on the other side of the river, but there was a narrow bridge we could walk over. He pulled over and parked in a clearing, and we all got out of the car.

The old house was visible from here, though partly hidden by trees. I couldn't believe the two-story shack built on cinder blocks was still standing. When Dennis and his housemate Bill occupied it, the place had no heat, and some of the windows were knocked out and covered in plastic sheets. When the snow melted after a storm late that winter, the place had flooded. That's when they had decided to move out.

We began the trek across the bridge. "I'm pretty sure this was the original road," said Dennis.

"Was it this narrow?" I asked. I put my arm around Jack, who walked slowly.

"Don't you remember? Only one car could cross at a time."

"Wow, Dad. I can't believe you lived this far away from campus and rode your bike to school."

"I only did that for a couple weeks," said Dennis. "That was before I moved in here—it was when I lived in another house up the road. I was crazy."

"Yeah, you were," I agreed. "Those two-lane roads were treacherous, and hilly."

"No shoulder, either," said Dennis. "I got run off the road at least once by an eighteen-wheeler."

"I'm sure you weren't wearing a helmet," I said.

Jack shook his head slightly. "The dark ages."

"Right," I said.

About halfway over the bridge, we were close enough to the house to see that somebody was living in it. At least, there were a few cars parked nearby.

"It looks like it could be a meth lab," said Dennis.

"I'm sorry, Dad, but can we go back now? I'm getting really tired. I think I'd like to take a nap today."

"Sure," said Dennis. "Let's go. The trip down this narrow memory lane is over."

Back at the hotel, Jack stretched out on his bed. I took a basket full of dirty clothes and went to search for a Laundromat in town.

It wasn't hard to find one. The place was busy, but there were plenty of machines available. It was humid and smelled of detergent, sweat, and dirt. Children ran around in circles and young moms kept reeling them back in; there were even a few babies in worn, secondhand carriers. I put our clothes in a washer and sat down in a vinyl chair to wait.

I felt a brief sense of normalcy. Laundry was something I did at home: it was in my mom-job description. It was something helpful that I could do for us here. Then, once our clothes were clean and fresh, I could get back to the hotel, and to Jack.

I read while I waited, and when our clothes were dry, I folded them in the basket and drove back to the hotel. I walked to the elevator and saw Dennis sitting on a sofa in the lounge across from the restaurant, reading his book.

"What are you doing down here?" I asked.

"I thought I'd let him sleep. I think it's okay for him to be up in the room by himself, don't you?"

"But—"

"Why don't you go up and check on him? If you think you should stay with him, do. But if he's all right, maybe it's better if we let him sleep undisturbed. Do you agree?"

"Maybe. If I do, I'll be back down in a bit."

"Okay. Whatever you think."

A minute later, I entered the dark room and set the basket down. Jack was breathing regularly and was fast asleep. I hesitated for a few minutes, then went to join Dennis downstairs. We could check on him after thirty minutes or so.

Before I left, I wrote a note in big letters saying where we were. I didn't want him to wake up, not find anyone with him, and not know where we were.

Chapter 12

July 4 - 6

You never know how strong you are
until being strong is the only choice you have.

– Bob Marley

The next morning, we decided to go to mass, then go to Chapel Hill for brunch. Using our car's navigation system, we tried to find the Catholic church in Durham that I had looked up, but the directions led us to a dead end.

"Let's head toward Chapel Hill," said Dennis. "If we don't see a church on the way, we can go to the Newman Center on campus."

The next mass at the Newman Center was scheduled to start soon, and, not finding another option, we pulled into the parking lot behind it. We walked in and found three chairs together on the right. The small room was filled with people; most were middle-aged or over, but a few students dotted the rows.

Jack was the tallest person in the room, and as we stood up at the beginning of mass, the bandage on the back of his head stood out like a big white gauzy thumb. After the readings and before communion, when the time came for petitions, people in the congregation spoke up, offering prayers for specific people. I silently prayed for Jack. During the homily, the priest talked about those healing from surgery, and all eyes were riveted to Jack. I reached for his hand and saw tears fall down his cheeks.

Then I pretty much lost it. I cried, wiped my face, and cried some more. A huge lump had formed in my throat and wouldn't go away. Somehow, we made it through communion, and as we started to leave, several people stopped Jack to wish him well.

"Wow," he said when we were back in the car. "That was really good. I'm glad we went."

"Me, too," said Dennis softly. "Now, hungry?"

He dropped Jack and me off in front of Top of the Hill restaurant, then went to park the car. We took the elevator up to the rooftop restaurant and were seated at a table. This place hadn't existed when Dennis and I were students, but in recent years we had dined here during happier visits to UNC.

After a tasty brunch, we decided to walk around a little again, this time to the Bell Tower and Kenan Stadium. We strolled through the quads and passed Wilson Library, but when we got to South Road, across from the Bell Tower, Jack asked Dennis if he could go back to town to get the car and pick the two of us up. "I'd rather not walk all the way back from here to Franklin Street, if that's okay."

"Sure," said Dennis. "I'll be right back." He gave me a kiss and trotted off.

We sat down on a stone wall and Jack checked his phone. A friend from high school, Ryan McManus, was a UNC student and was attending summer school. He and Jack had been trading messages. When Dennis drove up, we got in the car.

"He said he and his girlfriend are going to a movie this afternoon at a mall, and he invited us to meet them," Jack said.

"That sounds great," said Dennis. "So—Ryan knows why you're here in North Carolina and everything?"

"Yep. He's a good friend."

After a break at the hotel, we got to the cineplex early and found Ryan and his girlfriend waiting for us. Ryan was wiry, had a mess of dark hair, and stood a good six inches shorter than Jack. His girlfriend was a slim redhead and almost as tall as he was. He introduced her and himself to us.

"Dude, how're you doing?" he asked Jack.

"Better every day. I'm glad we could do this!"

"Yeah, me too," said Ryan. "How long you in town for?"

Jack glanced at me. "At least til Wednesday," I said. "That's his next appointment, when they get the results back."

"Good luck," said Ryan. "Let me know how things go, okay?"

"I will."

We bought our tickets and went inside to watch the action film. I didn't care what the show was—and I don't remember it—but I was thankful that Jack could rest in a dark theatre for a couple hours, and grateful for Ryan and his girlfriend, both of whom seemed kind.

After the movie, Dennis suggested that we eat dinner at a restaurant at the mall and invited the young couple to join us.

They conferred for a second and then Ryan spoke up. "Thanks, Mr. McDermott, but I think we're gonna get going." He turned to Jack. "Talk to you soon, okay?"

They gave each other a man-hug and Jack said goodbye to the girl. After they began to walk to the parking lot, Jack turned to Dennis.

"Could we go to Maggiano's for dinner, Dad?"

"Sure, whatever you want," said Dennis. We'd gone to an Atlanta Maggiano's for special occasions, so maybe Jack thought it was a stretch to ask. But we could afford it, and conveniently, it was only paces away. We ambled over and were seated at a square table. I ordered a glass of white wine. It was comforting to focus on things like ordering and enjoying food, and I was thankful that Jack's appetite was so good.

Over dinner, I thought about the last few days in the hotel and the way Jack had handled them. He, Dennis, and I had never spent so much time together; as the de facto middle child, he'd never had our undivided attention. He'd learned early to entertain himself, and to do what he wanted without being detected; we'd jokingly called him "under-the-radar-Jack." As a middle child myself, I related to his position in the family. Now, he was forced into being something he wasn't used to: the center of attention, and in a very unwelcome way.

Of course, he preferred to hang out with his friends, not his parents. No other nineteen-year-old he knew had to the way he did right now. Until the day we learned of the tumor, our relationship with him resembled that of most other parents and sons his age. We had loosened the rein on him over the past year, resisting the urge to hover during his freshman year at UGA. He'd kind of reinvented himself there, made lots of friends, and gotten involved in the campus improv group. He had also earned over a B average, kept the Hope Scholarship, and found a summer internship.

Then, on his first day home, his world had changed forever.

Here it was, eight weeks later, and he'd had two brain surgeries. He'd gotten over the shock and had let go of whatever anger he had had. Perhaps he was now in the bargaining stage of grief about his diagnosis—perhaps we all were: If we just did everything we were told, it would all work out.

But in my view, Jack had moved beyond that stage before we had arrived at Duke. He had gone through depression, too—actually, sadness. But that had been brief. Now, I felt he had come to the acceptance stage. What we would find out on Wednesday could change that, and it could throw him and all of us back into shock.

Which was something I didn't want to think about.

We hadn't discussed the worst case scenario of the pathology results: that the tumor might be a "bad" kind, like a glioblastoma—one with a low cure rate that could come back, and that might even kill him. Over the last few weeks, despite my earlier decision not to, I'd read up on the different types of brain tumors online. But each time I began reading, a feeling of dread formed in the pit of my stomach. Then I stopped reading and renewed my resolve to stay away from the Internet. I didn't know if Jack had read about them, but I hoped not. We would learn what kind of tumor it was soon enough, and then it wouldn't matter what other kinds there were.

Jack had shown incredible strength and a positive attitude, which gave me comfort, and which, truth told, didn't surprise me. He'd been a very loving, happy and grateful child. He had always made friends easily, adapting well when we moved across the country twice during his childhood. His older brothers had one another to fall back on and were each other's best friend. Academic success had come easily for them, and they had held their own on the field in track and cross country. Annette had competed in dance and sports, and was also a high academic achiever; she was the most organized kid we had. All four children had worked very hard in school. But Jack had had to work harder than the others.

He'd faced several challenges and disappointments—mental and physical—during his young life. At nine months old, he'd been diagnosed with a heart murmur; a test showed he was born with a hole in his heart. However, at age four, it had closed on its own. As a toddler, he had almost died from an allergic reaction on a trip to Disney World. Then there was the finger in the door accident.

In grade school, he'd had teachers who had been frustrated with him and disciplined him for just being a boy: disorganized, messy, and rumpled. In high school, he didn't make the basketball team, despite his height and his contribution to a winning middle school team. With no experience in football, he had signed up for the team, given it everything he had, and been awarded little playing time. He'd found a passion in acting, but had to settle for the Chorus and supporting roles when he wanted the lead. He'd even gotten screwed by a tough (and perhaps unfair) zero-tolerance school policy when he handed in a big paper one day late.

Dennis and I had continually backed him up and encouraged him, but he always seemed to get bad breaks. He'd been born on a Wednesday, and more than once I'd feared that his life really would be "full of woe," as the poem went. Because of what we had been through together this summer, the three of us were closer than we'd ever been. He had leaned on us, and I thought he was grateful that he could. He also got that Dennis and I had been going through our own grief. He understood how much we loved him, and he seemed strengthened by it.

He would have to continue to be strong, though. He had no other choice.

* * *

Monday morning was July 5 and a legal holiday. We hadn't paid much attention to Independence Day, other than listening to fireworks going off in the distance after we got back to the hotel room. Dennis planned to go into a local SunTrust branch on

Tuesday to catch up at the office; he'd been balancing work demands as best he could for almost a week now. But today he was off: banks were closed.

At Jack's suggestion, we went to a nearby Waffle House for breakfast, then headed back to Chapel Hill. Lunch was at Breadmen's on Rosemary Street; the place had moved since we were students, and it was different now. We'd eaten out so much that it was getting increasingly hard to control my calories. However, I was thankful that we could afford it with the money we had budgeted for our Texas vacation; it made things that much easier. That afternoon, we hung out in the hotel room for a while. Jack popped the movie UP into his laptop, and he and I sat on the bed and watched it together. I had seen it a few months earlier, and I braced myself for his reaction at the beginning, when the wife died.

Death wasn't something I wanted him to think about, even in an animated film.

But the story was wonderful, and he loved it. With his sweet, innocent nature, I wasn't surprised. That evening, at Dennis' suggestion, we went to a Durham Bulls baseball game.

It was a lot easier and much cheaper to go to this game than it was to a Braves game. The parking garage was conveniently close to the stadium, and our seats were just a few rows up from first base. We could see the players well and easily watch the action. It was a prime location to catch a foul ball, too—something that every boy and man longed to do. Jack and Dennis had rarely had a chance to do that at Turner Field. It was warm, but not unbearable: clouds passed overhead from time to time, shading us at regular intervals. After a few innings, Dennis went to get some snacks.

Then, sometime during the middle of the game, a fly ball headed toward us. We looked up and watched it rise and then begin to drop, right over our heads. Neither Dennis nor Jack had a baseball glove. For a split second, I thought the ball would come down on top of Jack's head.

Crack! Thankfully, a fan in the row behind us caught it. Jack had moved away, and Dennis had moved toward it. In other circumstances, Jack would have gone for it, glove or no.

"Wow, Dad! I thought the ball was going to hit me!"

"I was afraid of that for a second, too. The one time you don't want a foul ball to come to you, it does!"

"I know!"

Not long after, Jack asked if we could bag the rest of the game and go back to the room. "I'm just really tired."

I was fine with leaving early, and I wasn't shocked that he was so beat. He'd been through so much in the past week that it was remarkable he'd been able to do this much. All his life, he had been a "sleeper"—he'd needed a minimum of eight hours.

"No problem," said Dennis. "Let's go."

* * *

The next day, after breakfast in the hotel restaurant, Jack and I took Dennis to a SunTrust branch and dropped him off. Jack and I planned to go to Chapel Hill, and we would pick Dennis up later.

"I've got a suggestion about what to do this morning," I said when we were alone in the car.

"What?"

"Well, you know how we went to see the house where Dad lived in college?"

"Yeah?"

"When I was a senior, and he had already graduated, I lived on Cameron Avenue, just down from the Carolina Inn. The house is still there and it looks like people are living in it. Would you like to drive over? I'd like to take a picture of it."

"Okay, sure."

A couple minutes later, we pulled into a parallel parking space on Cameron, across the street from my old house at 307. The wood two-story house had been kept up and was painted a mint shade of green. We got out of the car and stood on the sidewalk while I took a photo.

Then I had an idea. "You know, what if I go over there, knock on the door, and tell whoever answers that I lived there in college? Would that be weird?"

He shook his head. "Not at all. Do it. I'll go with you."

I just loved Jack's spontaneous, why-not attitude—it reminded me of me, sometimes. Before I lost my courage, we were standing on the porch and I had rung the bell. Jack stood next to me, wearing a University of Georgia T-shirt.

A short, pretty blonde girl opened the door. I introduced myself and explained why we had come.

"Oh, that's so cool," she said. "I'm in summer school, but I live here during the year too with five other girls. Would you like to come in and look around? It's relatively clean right now."

"I'd love to," I said, surprised. "Are you sure you don't mind?"

"Not at all. Come in."

"I'm Jack," he said brightly. "I go to the University of Georgia. We're up here for some surgery I had at Duke." He pointed to his head.

"Hi. I'm Chelsea. How are you doing now?"

"Much better, thanks." He grinned.

For the next few minutes, Chelsea showed us around the house. It was in much better shape than the way I remembered it in 1981. I recognized the floor plan, marveled at the modern kitchen appliances, and explained how things used to look, even though neither she nor Jack seemed interested.

"My room was on this level, near the kitchen."

"That's my room," said Chelsea. "Come in. I'll show it to you."

We followed her and I let Jack precede me. Her bedroom was furnished with a double bed, a desk, and a chest of drawers; the decor shouted "college girl." When I had lived there, it had been sparsely furnished, with few decorations.

A flirty air soon established itself between Jack and Chelsea. I was sure she thought he was cute, his big bandage notwithstanding. They kept chatting and smiling at each other as we moved through the other rooms. There were two bedrooms on the main level and four upstairs. At the top of the stairs, I motioned toward the second bedroom on the left.

"That's where my housemates and I watched the famous 'there-you-go-again' debate between Reagan and Carter!" I exclaimed. "The girl who lived in that room had a TV." Neither of them was impressed.

Back downstairs, we made our way to the front door and I thanked Chelsea for inviting us in and showing us around.

"Good luck," she said to Jack.

"Thanks," he said, grinning again. "It was great to meet you."

We didn't stay in Chapel Hill much longer, and in the afternoon, Jack took a nap before it was time to pick up Dennis. For dinner, we went to Crook's Corner in Carrboro, the town next to Chapel Hill. The restaurant had also moved from its earlier location, and it had changed considerably: a former barbecue joint, it was now an upscale, eclectic restaurant with a much healthier menu. I was happy to find lighter choices than what I'd expected, though. I had eaten fries–and whatever else I wanted–as a stress-reliever more often than I should have recently.

We got back to the hotel early and as we walked into the lobby, my cell phone rang. It was a local number that I didn't recognize. I answered it and was connected to the Duke Brain Tumor Center.

"Mrs. McDermott? We wanted to give you some news before your appointment tomorrow."

"Yes?" I said, motioning to Dennis and Jack to stop and wait.

"The pathology results show that your son's tumor is a germinoma. Which is very good."

"A germinoma," I repeated, smiling at the guys.

"The doctor will discuss everything with you tomorrow, but we just wanted to let you know now, as we know you've been waiting for several days."

"Thank you."

"We'll see you all tomorrow morning."

I hung up, and the three of us high-fived each other. "That's the kind Dr. Tomaras thought it was, isn't it?" said Dennis. "The best kind."

"Right," I said. "I'm going to let Kathy O'Barr know, okay?"

"Sure," said Jack.

I left her a message to call me. A few minutes later, she did, and I relayed the information. "Julie," she said. "That's *terrific* news! You guys should be jumping for joy!"

Chapter 13

July 6 - 10

"It's always something, to know you've done the most you could. But don't leave off hoping, or it's of no use doing anything. Hope, hope, to the last!"

– Charles Dickens, *Nicholas Nickleby*

Back in the hotel room, Dennis called his mother to let her know the pathology results. With her medical background, she knew what the possibilities were and what they meant. This evening, the family was gathered for dinner at Dennis' brother Kevin's house.

"That's fantastic!" I heard Mary say, then repeat the news to the crowd of uncles, aunts and cousins. "We're all cheering down here! Tell Jack we're thrilled, and we love him."

"I will," said Dennis. "We've already told him that depending on what we find out at tomorrow's appointment, we're going to visit for Thanksgiving."

"Wonderful," said Mary.

I called my parents next and told them about the pathology results. "It's the best possible news, so we're really happy. We may be able to head home tomorrow. I'll let you know."

I answered a few of their questions, but hung up quickly, since we'd be seeing them soon. I was afraid they might bring up something negative they could have read, or even just share their worries. I wanted to focus on the positives only, for now.

The next morning, we ate a quick breakfast and left for Duke. We parked in the garage next to the Clinic and walked across the long pedestrian bridge to the Brain Tumor Center. Jack was called into an exam room, and a nurse checked his vital signs and changed his dressing.

She glanced at me. "You got the message about it being identified as a germinoma, didn't you?"

"Yes." I smiled.

"It's great news," she said, then turned to Jack. "Everything looks good around your incision. Your parents must have been taking good care of you since you left the hospital."

He glanced at us. "Yeah, they have."

"How does your neck feel?" she asked.

"A lot better. It doesn't feel stiff or sore anymore."

"Good. You must have been moving it around, then."

"I guess."

She laughed. "Well, Dr. Vredenburgh will be in to see you shortly. We call him Dr. V around here."

"Will I see Dr. Friedman?"

"Not this morning. Dr. V will be in to see you in a few minutes."

Dr. James Vredenburgh introduced himself, shook our hands and exuded optimism, saying germinomas were known to have a cure rate of over 90 percent.

Jack gave him a measured look. "So—I'm not cured yet? Even though the tumor's gone, I'm not done?"

Dr. V paused for a second. "Dr. Friedman was able to remove virtually all of your tumor. But there are some microscopic tumor cells that he wasn't able to extract because they are very close to your optic nerves. Once you've healed from the surgery—and it looks like you're doing well—you're going to need radiation therapy to kill the remaining cells."

Jack dropped his eyes, a dejected look settling on his face. "But I thought it was over."

"Jack," said the doctor, "no, it's not over. You have cancer. But the good news is that the type of cancer you have is curable. You only need twenty-five radiation treatments. They don't hurt, and they don't take long—only about seven to ten minutes. The first one will take the longest, because that's when they fit you and get you started. After that, it'll be a breeze. But you'll have to go in every weekday for five weeks."

I recalled my friend Susan telling me that the hardest thing about radiation was just getting there every day.

"Where should he go?" asked Dennis.

"We can do it here. But you live in Atlanta, don't you?"

"Yes," I said.

"You can do it there. No problem."

"When do I start? Next week?"

Dr. V shook his head. "Not that soon. We need to give you a little more time to heal. Your family doctor can remove your stitches in a few days. You and your parents need to contact the radiation doctors in Atlanta and ask to get you on their schedule, starting the week after next. We'll work together with them." The doctor looked at a big paper calendar on the wall. "We could shoot for you to start a week from Monday, which is July nineteenth, and you'd be through by Friday, August twentieth."

Jack gave me a look. I knew what he was thinking: classes at UGA started on August 16.

"Given this," I said, "will Jack be able to go back to school in the fall?"

"When does school start?"

"The middle of August," said Jack, looking crestfallen. His eyes had filled with tears. "I'd have to miss the first week of class. So, I guess—"

"Wait a minute," said Dennis, turning to Jack. "Athens is just over an hour away. What if we schedule your treatments early in the morning, and Mom and I pick you up and take you back that last week? You said you don't have morning classes."

Jack raised his eyebrows and looked from Dennis to me. "You guys would do that for me? Commute to Athens every day?"

"Of course," I said, smiling. "It would only be a week, anyway." I'd have done it the whole twenty-five days if need be.

Dr. V brightened. "I don't see any problem with that plan. Let's make it happen."

"Great!" said Dennis. "We'll make it happen, Jack!"

* * *

Dr. V green-lighted us to drive home that afternoon, but before we left, a thirty-something social worker with dark hair and a sympathetic smile ushered us into a small conference room. We sat down at a round table and she handed me a folder about the Preston Robert Tisch Brain Tumor Center.

She outlined the folder's contents, then asked Dennis and me about our experience at Duke, and how we were managing the financial, psychological, and emotional stress. We assured her we could handle the costs that insurance didn't cover, and that, though not perfect, our marriage was strong. We also told her we had a close relationship with Jack, and we were encouraged by his determination and gratitude.

As she talked, I thought about the many cancer patients and their families she met with who weren't doing as well. She said that finances could become a major issue, and health care costs could be overwhelming. If family relationships were already shaky, the stress could be too much. A child's serious illness might drive a wedge in a marriage, and sometimes that resulted in separation or divorce.

Dennis and I glanced at each other. During our twenty-eight years together, we had been through our share of stress, and then some. Early on, we had weathered severe financial problems; later, we had dealt with many difficult issues during our kids' teenage years. However, we'd never fallen prey to blame and had chosen instead to lean on each other. But we'd never faced a serious illness, nor lost a loved one. As we walked out of there, I hoped our marriage was as strong as we both believed.

Minutes later, Dennis spoke as we drove away. "Hey! I see the hospital entrance in the rearview mirror!"

"And?" said Jack.

I turned back and looked at him. "Remember what the anesthesiologist said about most people's favorite memory? Seeing Duke Hospital in their rearview mirror?"

"Um—not really."

I glanced at Dennis. "Well, me and Dad do. It *is* a pretty sight."

We checked out of the hotel and got on the road back to Georgia. In the car, I called my parents and sent emails to my friends. My heart was full of hope.

* * *

We got home on Wednesday night, and the next morning, I called the radiation oncology department at St. Joseph's Hospital. St. Joe's was just around the corner from our neighborhood and across the street from Northside, where Jack had had the shunt surgery. I wasn't sure if Northside did radiation, but I knew St. Joe's did, and we thought it was the ideal place.

I talked to a receptionist who said St. Joe's could see him the next week. Later that day, I got a call from Duke.

"Mrs. McDermott? This is Duke Clinic calling with a doctor on the line from your son's oncology team here."

The hairs on the back of my neck stood up. What if they had found something else on the pathology results? What if they had made a mistake? "Okay."

"One moment, please."

I waited, and then an oncologist whose name I don't recall now—it wasn't Dr. V, though—said they'd heard from St. Joe's.

"Yes. I called this morning, and he has an appointment there next week. It's close to our home."

"Well, that's great, but the problem is, that's not where we want Jack to go for radiation."

"Oh. Why not?"

"It's not that St. Joseph's isn't a great place. It is. But we'd like for your son to go to Emory instead. We've worked with the radiation doctors at Emory for many years. Since you're in Atlanta, that's where we want Jack to go."

"Okay," I said, still a bit baffled. Emory had a good reputation, but so did St. Joe's. However, we had had no personal experience with either. "But—"

"Let me put it this way," cut in the doctor. "If Jack were the son of someone on our team—someone who needed to be in Atlanta for radiation—he'd go to Emory. No question about it. That's where he needs to go. We've already given them a call, so they're expecting to hear from you."

"Okay. Thank you very much. I'll cancel our appointment and make one at Emory."

I hung up and considered his words. This was important enough for Duke to call today, after they had heard from St. Joe's. I was a little frustrated that Dr. V hadn't specified Emory in the first place. I knew Emory was the best in town, but until now, I didn't realize that it was our only real choice. That, to survive, Jack needed the best. A pang of fear hit me and settled in my stomach, and the worry I had pushed away began to resurface.

I called Emory and learned that the radiation oncologist, Dr. Natia, could see him on Monday at 9 a.m., and another physician on the team wanted to see him Wednesday. Then, two days later, he was to have another MRI. Per Dr. V's instructions, he would begin radiation on Monday, July 19.

"The first appointment will take a while," said the receptionist. "After that, you'll be in and out in less than twenty minutes a day."

"Can we schedule his appointments for early morning?"

"You can talk to Dr. Natia about that, but I don't see a problem."

Later, I told Jack and Dennis about the new plan.

"Well, Emory's not as convenient, but if that's what Duke wants, that's what we'll do," said Dennis.

"They pretty much insisted. Emory's not too far, anyway."

"Thanks, Mom and Dad. I really appreciate everything you guys are doing."

"Oh, honey," I said. "Don't worry about it. We love you. Whatever it takes, we're going to do it."

* * *

Over the next few days, we kept cleaning Jack's incision and changing the bandage, and he tapered off his pain meds. Tom

O'Barr planned to come over on Saturday afternoon to remove the stitches.

Brian and Annette flew home on Friday, and Mom and Dad went to pick them up. When they got home around six, everyone came in to see Jack. Both grandparents gave him a big hug.

Annette reached in her bag and pulled out a card. "Here, Jack. This is from the family in Texas."

"Thanks." Jack took the card, opened it and sat down in the den to read it. I stepped over and watched his eyes well up.

"Are you okay?" I asked.

"Yeah. It's just–wow. This really means a lot."

"Do you mind if I read it after you?"

"No. Here you go."

All of his aunts, uncles, cousins and his grandmother in Texas had signed the get well card. It was covered with twenty-five handwritten messages like the following:

Missed you at the Classic and Pizza Cook-off. Next year for sure! Glad everything went well and hope to see you soon!

Get well man and make your way to Texas to get whooped in some poker and golf. Missed you man.

Hi Jack!! I'm sooooo glad you're doing good!!! Really wish you could have joined us...can't wait til next year. Love you.

Hurry up and get better soon. We miss you lots.

Get well soon, Jack! Hang in there, man!

Wish you could have been here. Can't wait to go to Choctaw over Thanksgiving.

Don't change your favorite color from Carolina blue to Blue Devil blue.

We love you.

"Gosh, what a nice thing to do," I said, feeling touched and a bit overwhelmed at the outpouring of love and concern.

"Can we frame this, Mom?"

"Sure, sweetie."

Later, we picked up our *Lost* DVD and watched another episode together, escaping into the fictional world of characters Sawyer, Desmond and Jack, and trying to follow the time-travel storyline. That night, *my* Jack went right to sleep.

The next afternoon, Tom came over to take out his stitches. Dennis and I hovered nearby as Tom carefully removed the bandage. The stitches were dark and thick, but the skin around them looked pink and healthy. A stubby patch of hair had begun to grow back.

"This won't take long," said Tom. He looked at Jack. "I *promise*, it won't hurt."

"I've heard that before," said Jack. "So it's hard to believe you."

"Trust me."

I believed him, but I chose not to watch.

A minute later, he was done. "There. Now I can say I've removed stitches from a surgery performed by Dr. Allan Friedman." He smiled. "You all right, buddy?"

"Yep. You were right. What does it look like back there?"

"It's all good," said Tom. "You can get it wet in the shower. You may want to get a haircut to even it out, but when it grows out, you won't be able to see the scar."

Jack went to a bathroom to check it out in the mirror while Dennis and I thanked Tom and said goodbye. A few minutes later, Jack came back and asked if I would take him to Great Clips. He wasn't clear to drive until he was off pain medication.

While we were out, Dennis went to the airport to pick up Keegan, who was staying until Thursday. When they got home, all three boys played pool in the basement, and then we had a family dinner.

When I went to bed that night, I was thankful to have everyone back in the nest, even if only for a few days.

Chapter 14

July 12 - 16

You couldn't relive your life, skipping the awful parts,
without losing what made it worthwhile.
You had to accept it as a whole – like the world,
or the person you loved.

– Stewart O'Nan

On Monday morning, July 12, Jack and I headed to Decatur for his appointment at Emory. On the way, he brought up something he'd asked Tom about on Saturday.

"He said he didn't think I'd lose my hair, but he wasn't sure."

"I asked Mrs. O'Barr about that, too," I said. "She said the same thing. But I thought I also heard one of the doctors at Duke say he didn't think you would lose any."

"Really? Good. I hope he's right. I'd rather not go back to school bald."

We arrived at the Winship Cancer Institute and drove up to the valet. I was fine with paying the eight bucks today; we would park in the garage starting tomorrow. We got out of the car and took the elevator down to Radiology, located in the basement. Following the signs, we turned left and walked down a long wide corridor toward a curved check-in counter. Jack gave the receptionist his name and she took his insurance card.

"Have a seat. Someone will call you shortly."

We walked to the waiting room opposite the counter and sat down. About twenty people occupied the orange vinyl chairs lined up against the walls. A large aquarium in the center anchored the room and divided it into two spaces. I surveyed the small group and decided who was the patient and who was the caregiver. A few people sat by themselves.

Everyone was older than Jack, and most were close to my age or older. One person was in a wheelchair and another was missing half of his jaw. A few were bald, and one woman was wearing a wig. Most people were reading or watching the television bolted to the wall high in one corner, but a few were chatting with each other.

I looked at the time: it was just after nine o'clock. I wondered if the same group of people was here each day at this time, and whether we would soon join them. Some were downright scary-looking. I wondered how Jack felt in their midst. Did they frighten him? Did they depress him? They certainly did unnerve me, and I wasn't the patient. I felt guilty for my reaction, but I couldn't help it. Then I thought about how everyone in here had been healthy at some point in the past.

Just like Jack.

"John McDermott?" called a nurse.

Jack told her his nickname, which she wrote on a form, and we followed her into a maze of metal and magnets. Sets of pale curtains lined our path; some were closed, and some were parted to reveal padded tables and grim contraptions. We passed a long glass window in front of a huge monitor showing graphs and tables. Our trip ended in a wide boxy space where four closed doors dotted the corners.

"You'll be in here," said the nurse, opening the first door on the right. "Dr. Natia will be in to see you in a few minutes."

The doctor's name was Dr. Esiashvili, but because it was so difficult to pronounce, everyone called her by her first name. Another nurse came in to measure Jack's height and weight and take his blood pressure. She handed him some forms to fill out.

He gave me a questioning look. "Would you?"

"No problem." I had gotten really good at filling out medical forms.

"Too bad you can't just do those once, for everybody."

I nodded. "Yep, that would be great. Nothing's easy, though."

Dr. Natia came in a few minutes later. She was at least ten years younger than me, and several inches shorter, with olive skin, dark almond-shaped eyes, and shoulder-length hair. She shook our hands and asked us to tell Jack's story from the beginning. Together, we did, trying not to take too long, but also trying not to leave out anything important. When Jack came to the part about going to Duke, she interrupted him and directed a question to me.

"Why didn't you come to Emory? We do brain surgeries here, and you *live* here."

I paused for a second, feeling a bit uncomfortable and put on the spot. Then I shrugged and looked directly at her. "We just wanted to go to Duke."

She gave me a look, and Jack took the cue to continue. "They advised us to come here to Emory for radiation," he finished.

"Yes, we've talked to the team there," said Dr. Natia. "If I'm not mistaken, you're going to start on Monday, July nineteenth, and we agree with Duke that you'll need a total of twenty-five treatments. So, five weeks."

She explained that at his first appointment, Jack would be fitted for a mold, or mask, designed to hold his head perfectly still during radiation. "Do you have any questions for me right now?" she asked.

He looked right into her eyes. "Will I lose my hair?"

She took a second and let out a small sigh. "Yes, probably, though not right away. You won't lose any for the first couple of weeks. Then it will come out, but by that time you'll be almost done." She offered a weak smile.

He looked away, his eyes watery.

"Oh, come now," she said, a touch of reproach in her voice. "You're not a girl! You shouldn't feel sad about losing hair."

Jack looked back at her and then at me. I could see anger and hurt flash in his eyes, but he remained silent.

"Now, then. Anything else?" asked the doctor.

He shook his head.

"When will we see you again?" I asked.

"I'll see you about once a week. You know about the MRI scheduled for this Friday?"

"Yes," I said. "What time?"

"You'll find out at your appointment on Wednesday with Dr. Anna Janss. She'll go over all of that with you." Dr. Janss' office was across the way from this one, in Egleston, one of the Children's Healthcare of Atlanta hospitals. Even though Jack was over eighteen and was a legal adult, cancer patients up through age twenty-one were seen by pediatric oncologists. Dr. Natia explained that this was an advantage for Jack: he would get extra personal attention, and MRIs would be a little easier.

"If you don't have any more questions, I'll see you next week. Good luck."

We wound our way back to the desk and checked out.

"Did you valet park? I can stamp your ticket," said the receptionist.

I gave it to her and learned that during Jack's treatments, we could valet park every day, and she would validate the ticket—it was something they did for all radiation patients. It was a nice surprise, and a small but important expression of care and concern. We took the elevator up to the lobby. When we stepped off, my phone downloaded several email messages—there was no service in the basement. I also had some missed calls. I checked the messages, and one made me furious.

Evidently, our reupholstered chairs and sofa that were scheduled to be delivered this morning hadn't been, even though Brian was home and knew to expect them. The message said that the delivery people had arrived and called me, and when I hadn't answered, evidently they chose not to ring the doorbell to see if anyone was home, and then just left. Now they couldn't come back until next week.

It wasn't that my life depended on getting that furniture delivered that day. This was just a screw-up, and I shouldn't have allowed it to upset me. But instead of letting it go, I did the opposite. The fact that they drove to our house, but hadn't even bothered to ring the bell, pushed me over the edge.

It was the final straw of stress that I couldn't handle, and I snapped.

I called the person in charge before the valet brought my car up. Then I let loose with a tirade, emphasizing that there was no phone service in the radiation center, and that, since I had previously confirmed the time, the delivery people should have rung the doorbell. For all they knew, I could have been at home with a dead phone battery. I finished ranting, but didn't succeed in getting them to return with the furniture.

When I hung up, Jack blurted out that he was upset that Dr. Natia had chastised him for caring about losing his hair.

"Well," I said, still fuming about the delivery mixup, "you've got to admit, it has to be worse for girls."

He gave me a look of disbelief. "So you're saying, because I'm a guy, I'm not supposed to care?"

"Jack—"

"Are you *kidding* me, Mom?"

"But—"

"God, Mom! It's not just the hair—it's about my feelings! Who is that doctor to tell me how to feel? How does she know what I've been through?"

I looked at him. "Well, maybe she sees so many patients that—"

"I don't care. You don't understand. I'm allowed to have feelings. She can't tell me how to feel. Nobody can." He turned back and stared straight ahead, tears welling in his eyes.

I was shocked at how hurt he was, and astonished at his display of emotion. Then I remembered that, though Jack was 100 percent male, he was also sensitive, like my dad. Learning about the hair loss had been harsh, and to make things worse, he'd been admonished for getting upset about it. Rather than showing sympathy, I'd ignored him and had exploded about an insignificant, minor issue. Then, I'd rejected his feelings and had defended the doctor's words.

All of a sudden I remembered something I'd read online about the location of his tumor. It had been deep in his brain, near the amygdala, believed to be the emotional seat of the brain. It was responsible for emotional tranquility and relationships, even decision-making. If it was damaged, a person would have major problems coping with life.

Since his tumor had been sitting there, who knew what problems it could have caused? My mind flashed to memories of the more frequent than normal phone calls and texts I'd gotten from him last spring. At the time, I had decided he was fussy and upset due to allergies. When he got on allergy medication but still seemed agitated, I'd assumed he was going through something socially. I was glad he had his summer internship lined up, and I'd hoped he'd feel better and be able to relax over the summer.

Boy, was I wrong—it wasn't allergies or social issues. All that time, his tumor had been sitting there, and it was about to change his life. Now it seemed obvious that the stress he'd been going through was caused by the tumor growing in his head and pushing against his brain tissue. And who knew *how* long that had been going on—and what the effects had been?

But ever since the day we learned of his brain tumor, he'd somehow been able to cope with everything that was thrown at him. He *was* entitled to his own feelings, and there was a limit to what anybody could take. Though he didn't know what it was like to be a girl, Dr. Natia—and I—didn't know what it was like to be a guy. To be him. Finding out in such a cavalier way that he would lose his hair right before he began his sophomore year in college—and being chastised for his reaction—was more than harsh.

It was cruel.

"Jack," I said softly, "I'm sorry. You're absolutely right. You can feel however you want to about it, and no one gets to judge you."

He glanced at me, his face frozen, then turned away. I'd gotten good at reading his expression, and since he often wore his heart on his sleeve, it wasn't difficult.

"I mean it," I continued. "I didn't put myself in your place when she told you that you shouldn't feel sad. Then, after I got those messages about the delivery screw-up, I lost it. I didn't think about you anymore. I'm really sorry."

He looked at me again, as if gauging my sincerity. "Fine."

We drove on without a word, and I wondered how long it would take him to get over his anger toward me. It might not be soon—he'd dealt with a mountain of stress—and he was probably at his limit.

When we entered the neighborhood, he broke the silence. "Mom, it's okay. You get how it made me feel, though, right?"

"Yes. And—of course you get to feel however you want to."

He sighed. "Well, I don't like knowing I'm gonna lose my hair, but I guess I don't have any choice. I love you."

"I love you, too, honey." My eyes began to brim with tears. "Let's just take it a day at a time, okay?"

"Okay."

That evening, he played pool with his brothers. Keegan asked if he could go to the next appointment with us.

"Sure," said Jack. "That would be great."

* * *

On Wednesday morning, the three of us drove down to Dr. Janss' office at the Aflac Clinic at Egleston, located on the building's fourth floor. Jack checked in while Keegan and I found seats in the waiting room. It was filled with children and their parents; most kids were under twelve. My heart rose to my throat as I glanced around the room. Many of the kids were bald, and some were handicapped. All of them looked very sick. When Jack's name was called, we followed the nurse to an exam room. His height, weight, and blood pressure were measured, and this time, the nurse took a blood sample. Then we were shown to an exam room to wait for Dr. Janss.

Jack sat on the exam table and Keegan and I hovered next to him. A few minutes later, the doctor entered and introduced herself. Then she tested Jack's gross motor skills and examined his eyes.

Dr. Janss was closer to my age than Dr. Natia was, and she had a mom-like way about her. She had dark blonde hair that grazed her shoulders and that didn't look particularly styled, and her deep-set eyes had a twinkle in them. She explained that she and Dr. Natia met with a team of doctors each week to discuss their patients. After Jack started radiation on Monday, he would come over to Dr. Janss' office once a week for blood work and an examination.

He wasn't thrilled at this news, but he took it in stride. He gave short, direct answers to her questions and insisted that he felt "fine." Dr. Janss knew of our plan to commute from Athens for his last week of treatment, and, implying that she wasn't sure she agreed, she cautioned Jack that he might experience fatigue this fall and "hit a wall."

I knew he was determined to go back to school, come what may, because Dr. V had said he could. In as few words as possible, he told her so, no matter what the side effects were or how hard radiation might be. It was a nonnegotiable.

"Okay," said Dr. Janss. "Then you'll need to take a light class load."

"Fine," he said curtly. "I'll drop a class."

"Okay," she said. She threw a glance my way and then trained her eyes back on Jack. "Here's something else you should do: get online or call your school's Disability Office and register with them."

Jack shook his head. "I'm not disabled."

Dr. Janss gave him a look. "That's not what I'm talking about. Your brain has just been traumatized by two surgeries, and it's about to undergo another trauma with radiation."

"Still—"

"Listen to me," she said, her voice a bit aggravated. "If you'd been in a serious car wreck this summer, had recovered, and could go back to school, I would tell you to do the same thing. Registering with the Disabilities Office doesn't mean you're disabled. It just means you're letting your school, and professors, know what's happened in your life. There are a lot of things they can do to help you when you get back to school."

"Like what?"

"Like, for example, help with note-taking. Someone can take notes for you—"

"I don't need that."

"They'll also alert your teachers before the semester begins—"

"I don't want anyone's pity."

"—and they may give you extra time when you're taking tests."

Jack cocked his head. "Really? Wouldn't that be unfair?"

She shook her head. "Not at all. Your brain is working just fine, but like I said, it's been traumatized. I'm not sure if they'll allow you extra time, or if you'll need it. But even if you don't, it would be a good idea to find out, don't you think?"

"Jack," I said, "I agree with Dr. Janss. Let's just look into it, okay?"

"Fine. We can look into it, but that's all."

Dr. Janss threw an exasperated glance at me, and I gave her a nod. I listened as she began questioning him about his life: What was his major? Did he live in a dorm? Was he in a fraternity? Did he have a girlfriend? She was trying to get to know her patient, and he was bent on keeping his private life private.

She gave up and switched topics. "Now I want to mention something else, just in case Dr. Natia didn't, and that's this. Because of your tumor's proximity to your pituitary gland, radiation may affect your fertility someday later on, in the future. I know you're not thinking about this right now. But when you're ready to have kids someday, if you have any issues, there are things that can be done. Okay?"

Jack nodded, and I spoke up. "I think Dr. V at Duke mentioned that—or maybe it was one of the other oncologists."

She looked at me. "Good. Since he'll be seeing neurologists on an ongoing basis, it's something that you and they just need to remember. Now," she said, turning back to Jack, "let's talk about your MRI on Friday."

It would take place in the hospital's radiology department, located in the basement of this building. Even though they had his post-op MRI from Duke, performed hours after surgery, Emory wanted their own brain scan prior to beginning radiation. Keegan was flying back up north tomorrow, and Jack and I would come back here the following day for the MRI.

* * *

That night, Jack called me to come in his room to talk again before he went to sleep.

I took one look at his face and could see that he was troubled. It was frozen with fear. "What's the matter, babe?"

"It's something the doctor said today—about what radiation could affect."

I sat down on the side of his bed. "You mean the fertility thing?"

"Yeah."

"But she explained that there are things they can do, when the time comes, remember?"

"It's not that, Mom."

"What is it, then?"

"My pituitary gland is in charge of hormones, right?"

"Yeah? So?"

"I thought they were doing radiation on my *brain*, not my—"
He pointed to the lower half of his body under the covers.

"They are. What are you saying?" I stopped. "Oh, you
thought—silly! Don't you remember high school science, and sex
education? Your pituitary gland is in your brain!"

"Oh, thank God! No, I forgot."

I shook my head. "Relax. No one's messing with your man-
hood!"

A sheepish look settled on his face, and he took a deep
breath and let it out. "Wow. That's a relief!"

* * *

The next day, we took Keegan to the airport.

"You'll be in my prayers," he said to his brother at the security gate. "Keep me updated, okay?"

"I will." Jack gave him a man-hug. "Thanks for coming
down."

"I can come back anytime," said Keegan. "Good luck."

Jack and I drove home, and on Friday, we were back at
Emory for the MRI.

"We're getting good at this," I said as we took the elevator
down to Radiology. "At least, *you* are."

Jack shrugged. "It gets easier every time."

I thought about a comment Dr. Tomaras had made to me
and Dennis back in May: that Jack would have many, many MRIs
in his life. He *had* gotten good at them—and he never complained.

Sitting next to him in the cramped Radiology waiting room,
I filled out yet another set of forms, making sure to check the
boxes indicating that Jack had a VPI shunt and titanium screws
in his head. Then I told the receptionist about them.

When his name was called, we walked in to a small exam
room. A nurse came in and gave him a list of movies to choose

from: he could watch a video during the MRI—one of the perks for pediatric patients. Another perk was a butterfly IV stick, which was a little easier, and a numbing gel at the site of it. I imagined what Jack's previous MRIs must have been like, and marveled at his toughness. Having to go through this just once would be too much for me, yet he had done it several times.

He *was* a Marine.

After they took him in, I pulled out my Kindle and read, and an hour later, we hastened home. Our next appointment was on Monday morning at nine o'clock at the Winship Cancer Institute, where he would be fitted for the mask and have his first radiation treatment.

Chapter 15

July 18 - August 13

I like living. I have sometimes been wildly, despairingly, acutely miserable, racked with sorrow; but through it all I still know quite certainly that just to be alive is a grand thing.

— Agatha Christie

On Sunday afternoon, Jack said he wanted to go shopping for baseball caps. He had a red one he liked, but he wanted to buy a new one so that he would have two. "I'm going to start wearing one every day. That way, when my hair starts falling out, I'll look the same."

"Want me to go with you?" I offered. "We could go to the mall."

"Okay."

We drove to Lenox Square and found a store that sold ball caps in several sizes, emblazoned with dozens of team names. After browsing through them for a few minutes, he chose an off-white fitted cap with a dark red **A** on it, in the style of the Atlanta Braves baseball team. He put it on backwards. "This will go with anything."

I hadn't realized that was his goal, but it made sense, and wearing it backwards was the style, anyway. It would hide the back of his neck, which would be bare. He seemed resigned about the hair loss now; he knew he'd be wearing a cap for a while, and he wanted coverage. I didn't blame him.

Monday's appointment did take a long time, but afterward, Jack emerged from the bowels of the radiation treatment center smiling and happy.

"The nurses here are really nice–and pretty," he said as we headed toward the elevator. "I don't think I'll mind seeing them every day."

The valet brought the car up and we climbed in. Jack pulled his iPhone out of his pocket and turned to me. "Do you want to listen to my playlist on the way home?"

"Sure."

For the next twenty minutes, he played his favorite songs and sang along as he watched my reaction. Most were (clean version) hip-hop tunes. I liked several of them because of the lyrics and the music. Some kind of fit him and his journey, such as "Not Afraid," "Dead and Gone," and "All the Above." Some were just funny, like "Billionaire" and "Whatever You Like."

"We could do this every day, if you want," he said when the last song was over.

"That would be fun!"

We drove on in silence, and I looked over and smiled at him when we sat at a red light.

"What?" he said.

"Nothing. It's just that I'm glad you've already found something we can do on the drive. I'm flattered that you want to share your music with me, too."

He grinned. "I'm glad you like it. And since we're going to be together every day, why not?"

* * *

That Wednesday, my brother's youngest son Rory was turning a year old. He and his wife were having a party at their neighborhood pool and had invited us. Annette had a babysitting job that day, so she couldn't go, but Brian and Jack and I drove down after radiation and a quick change of clothes. I was looking forward to seeing everyone, and to doing something fun–and normal.

I was surprised that Jack didn't wear his cap, but I guessed that in front of family, he didn't care. With his short haircut, his scar from the shunt surgery showed prominently on the front of his head. His long scar in the back was visible, too. Hatless, he looked like a combat veteran, but he was all smiles as he walked down the steps to the pool entrance gate.

I don't remember much of the birthday party other than eating pizza while the kids played in the pool. I chatted with Mom and Dad and reported how well Jack had done with radiation. Everyone seemed comfortable around him, and no one said anything about his diagnosis or asked about what he was going through.

It was a welcome, pleasant break in our routine.

The next day after treatment, we walked across the drive to Egleston for his weekly appointment with Dr. Janss. We sat in the waiting room with all the children until a nurse called his name.

We squeezed into the closet-sized room, where the nurse drew his blood, weighed him and measured his height.

"Woo–wee, Mom!" she said to me. "Looks like your boy has grown some!"

I threw Jack a look. "He has? What's his height?"

"Six foot six!" She turned to another nurse sitting in front of a computer monitor. "Seventy-six inches."

"Wait a minute," I said, holding up a hand. "Five feet equals sixty inches, so six feet would be seventy-two. So, doesn't seventy-six inches equal six foot four?"

Jack and I exchanged glances, and I stifled a laugh. The nurse's cheeks reddened and she turned back to her colleague. "Six foot four." She turned to Jack. "Go down to exam room five and wait for the doctor." She turned around and busied herself with paperwork.

We walked down the hall and chuckled over what had just happened while we waited for the doctor.

"'*Your boy has grown some!*'" Jack parroted the nurse, then laughed. "'Seventy-six inches!'"

I laughed too. "I guess math isn't her strong subject."

A few minutes later, a tall, attractive blonde nurse came into the exam room and introduced herself. Her name was Maggie, and she had graduated from UGA a few years ago. She asked Jack questions about school and about how he was feeling. He was talkative and open. She said she would come in to see him each week before Dr. Janss, and would go over the results of his blood work with him.

Then she handed him a copy of today's results, explained what some of them meant ("fights infection, gives you energy"), and jotted down the target ranges. All were within range or better, and she had written A+++ at the bottom.

"Bye, now. See you next week!" she said and walked out the door, shutting it behind her.

"Wow," said Jack, looking at me. "You never know when or where you're going to meet a beautiful girl!"

I smiled. "That's true."

He turned toward the door with a sudden, uneasy look.

"What's the matter?" I asked.

"It's just—when Dr. Janss comes in today—and from now on—would you do me a favor?"

"What?"

"Well, I want to be done as soon as possible. So would you let me do the talking?"

"What if I have questions for her?"

He lifted his eyebrows. "She talks a *lot.* So, how about this: you just listen, and let *me* ask the questions. Then, at the end, if you have any questions I didn't ask, do it then. Okay?"

"Fine." It was a reasonable request, though I felt a bit uncomfortable being verbally restrained. "What if she talks directly to me, though, or asks me something?"

"Then answer her. But keep things short and specific, so we can get out of here, okay?"

"All right."

A few moments later, Dr. Janss entered and gave him a quick exam. As promised, I kept silent and let him handle it. Our visit was over in less than ten minutes, and Jack walked out with a spring in his step.

Each morning, on our way to Decatur and back, he played his tunes and we sang along together. Sometimes we stopped on the way back at the Starbucks at the corner of North Druid Hills and Briarcliff Roads. I was happy his appetite wasn't affected by radiation, and glad to buy him a pastry and caramel latte. At home, he usually ate a turkey sandwich and then took a nap or watched television; I was glad he slept when he was tired, and that he seemed able to keep his batteries charged.

One morning the next week, we were driving to Emory as usual when we almost crashed.

We were in the middle lane on Peachtree Road, and approaching the light at Dresden before our left turn at North Druid Hills. The light was green. A semitrailer truck in the long, left turn-only lane began to come into ours.

I didn't have time to honk the horn. We were right behind the truck's cab, and I might have been in his blind spot. The lane to our right wasn't clear, but the road was open ahead.

I floored the gas pedal and cleared the truck just as it finished changing lanes. Just ahead was the light at North Druid Hills. I got over in the left lane and slowed down.

I did all of this in seconds.

"Oh my God," said Jack. "Way to drive, Mom!"

"Jeez. That could have been bad, but it wasn't my fault."

"I know! That guy wasn't paying attention. He could have hit us, but you didn't let him."

"In any case, let's not have any other close calls. I can't handle it!"

On Thursday afternoon, July 29, Jack had a follow up appointment with Omni Eye Services, with whom Dr. Janss and Dr. Natia had been in touch. After radiation and lunch at home, we drove to the eye doctors' office in the Peachtree-Dunwoody Medical Center.

This time, a nurse summoned Jack and said he would be seeing Dr. Day, one of the older doctors in the group.

"What about Dr. Sturdy? That's who I saw before."

"Dr. Sturdy has moved to Colorado," came the response. "Don't worry–Dr. Day has seen all your records."

Dr. Day was more reserved than Dr. Sturdy, but Jack and I liked him. Jack told him an abbreviated version of what he had been through since our last visit to Omni, and Dr. Day listened closely. I wondered if he had ever seen another patient like him. He did all the same tests Dr. Sturdy had done, and showed Jack the results, including the picture of his retinas. They looked tons better this time–even we could tell the difference.

When we checked out, Dr. Day had us make a follow-up appointment for late October, and he wished Jack well.

On July 31, I wrote a handwritten note and sent it to Omni, and hoped they would share it with Dr. Sturdy.

Dear Dr. Day and Dr. Sturdy,

Enclosed are copies of the pathology reports from Duke in early July, and from the follow up MRI done at Emory most recently on my son Jack (John Dennis McDermott). I hope this is what you requested to complete your info on him.

Jack and I both want to thank you for all you did for him. Jack felt he got excellent care from you and was always treated respectfully, and I agree. It meant so much to us that Dr. Sturdy was willing to see Jack on such short notice on May 8. Dr. Sturdy was incredibly nice, making Jack feel comfortable and explaining everything. We wish him luck in Colorado and we are grateful to Dr. Day for taking over for Jack.

With gratitude,
Julia McDermott

The next week, Jack's blood work came in great again. A few days later, his hair began to fall out.

It had just started to grow in after the surgery, and now big patches were on his pillow.

"I wonder how long it'll take for it all to come out," he said to me.

"You could just get it all shaved off now."

"No. I'm going to start wearing my hat all the time, though."

He did, and it seemed to hasten the process. Before long, he was bald, and the bump and ridge of his shunt—and the scar around it—were visible again.

One day after our visit to Starbucks, we had a disturbing experience. As we walked to the car in the almost full parking lot, I had my keys in one hand and my coffee in the other. Using the remote, I unlocked the car. I was slightly ahead of Jack, who was walking toward the passenger's side.

All at once, I saw a man of about thirty years old walking straight toward me. He was under six feet tall, had scraggly long brown hair and was dressed in dirty, rumpled clothes. His eyes were crazy looking. An alarm bell rang inside my head. Was this guy about to do something?

A split second later, Jack was at my side, stretched to full height and leaning forward. "What do you need, dude?"

The man stopped abruptly, turned right and mumbled, "Nothing, man." He walked away. Then Jack and I got in the car and I locked the doors.

"Whoa," I said.

"You okay, Mom?"

"Yeah. But that guy scared me."

"He was weird."

"Gosh, though, thanks for what you did!"

"What'd I do?"

"You got him to back off! You rescued me!"

"Well, I wouldn't say—"

"No, really! If I had been alone—if you hadn't been there—well, even in the middle of the day like this, what if he had grabbed me or something?"

Jack shook his head. "I don't know, but—anyway, let's get out of here."

"Yeah, let's." I turned on the ignition and started to back out. "Thank you."

"You're welcome. Now, let me turn on some music."

As we listened, I thought about what had just happened. Realistically, what could have happened to me if Jack hadn't been there? If the guy had assaulted me, I would have screamed, but who knows if I would have been hurt?

Maybe he had only aimed to grab my keys and steal the car. Whatever his intention was, I was glad I'd had my son there. Jack had acted decisively and instinctively. All this time, I'd been trying to protect him, but he had pulled a role reversal and protected me from potential danger, even though he was fighting cancer.

What a good man he was.

* * *

Later that week, we encountered another radiation patient we hadn't seen before.

He was a thick man in his fifties or sixties, as tall as Jack and almost as bald. He didn't wear a hat, and he didn't have a companion. I supposed he had just started treatment; maybe very little hair was normal for him.

We were in the elevator when he hustled over to join us, and Jack held the door open for him.

"Thank you," said the man, nodding.

"You're welcome," said Jack. "Having a good day?"

The man chuckled a little and looked at Jack. "I guess so. But we *all* have cancer, though, right?" He smiled.

No one said anything as the elevator traveled up and the door opened. The man scurried off, and Jack and I trudged to the valet desk.

"God!" said Jack, his eyebrows raised. "I didn't like *that* guy!"

I looked up at him. "You mean—"

"'*We all have cancer!*'" Jack repeated. He shook his head.

I kept silent as we waited for our car. It was the first time anyone other than a doctor had said the word *cancer* to Jack. Dr. V had said, "you have cancer," but we had not. We had talked about the brain tumor, surgeries and radiation, but—without specifically agreeing on it—we hadn't ever said that word.

Right or wrong, it had worked.

We got in the car and I asked Jack what about it had upset him so much.

"It's not that I didn't know I have cancer—but all I did was ask if he was having a good day!"

"He *was* kind of flippant. People are weird."

"It's not just that, Mom. I mean, I know he's right. But what if I hadn't been ready to hear that from some stranger?"

"I guess it was part of that guy's way to cope."

"Yeah." He reached for his iPhone. "Oh, well. Fine. We all have cancer. But dude, I'm going to live!"

Chapter 16

August 14 - 31

Worry never robs tomorrow of its sorrow, but only saps
today of its strength.

– A. J. Cronin

On Saturday, Jack moved into an off-campus apartment with
three other guys for his sophomore year at UGA. Two of his
roommates had already moved in, and classes started on Monday.
He had already registered for the fall semester, and Dennis and I
had persuaded him to go to the Disability Resource Center online.
He had started the registration process, and he said that if he
changed his mind and decided to ask for any accommodations, he
would follow up with them and schedule an "intake" interview.

Before we left home for Athens that morning, the three of us
talked about the timetable for getting him to his 9 a.m. radiation
appointment over the coming week. Dennis planned to get on the
road early, arrive around 7:00, and try to get home before 8:30.
He would go to work, and I would take Jack to Emory and back

to Athens. Dennis and I suggested that he tell his roommates what was going on, since they could be sleeping when he left the apartment and might wake them.

As we pulled into the parking lot, Jack said he had a text from one the guys, Colby, who was at the apartment and would give him his key. The place was furnished, so there was little we had to carry in: a couple of suitcases, a small television for his room, and a box packed with some miscellaneous stuff. There was a big screen TV in the living area. Maybe because it was so hot, Jack wasn't wearing his ball cap.

A guy met us at the door of the ground-floor apartment, and Jack introduced us to Colby. He gave Jack a double take.

"Short haircut, dude!"

Jack mumbled something, grabbed his cap from his backpack, and put it on. Colby offered to help us carry things in.

"I think we got it," said Jack. "Thanks, though."

Colby retreated to the kitchen, and ten minutes later, we had all of Jack's belongings in his room. Dennis and I sat on the bed as he unpacked the box, looking for the cable cord for his TV. As he fumbled around, Colby walked by the entrance of the room and stopped. "Need some help?"

"Sure," said Jack, beckoning him to come in. After they got it set up, Jack looked around the room. "I can do the rest," he said to us. "You guys can head back now."

I looked at Dennis. If we were going to make sure that at least one of Jack's roommates knew about his early morning departures this week, now was the time.

Dennis cleared his throat. "Jack, remember how we said you should probably tell your buddies that I'll be coming to get you at seven o'clock this week?"

Jack nodded and looked at Colby, who wore an unblinking, quizzical expression.

"I have to go in to Atlanta to finish radiation at Emory," he said. "But it's just for five days."

"What?" said Colby.

"I had a brain tumor," said Jack. Dennis and I exchanged a quick glance, and I noted Jack's use of the past tense.

Colby started, looked up at Jack's head, then at us and back at Jack. "Gee, man. Sorry about the haircut remark."

"It's okay. I'll be wearing this for a while." He tapped the cap.

"You're okay, though?"

"Yeah. It's a long story. Anyway, after Friday, I'm done."

"Good. Hey, tell me if I can do anything."

"Sure. Thanks."

He walked out and Jack turned to me and Dennis. "Well, see you Monday."

I put my arms around him to give him a hug. "I love you, honey. See you then."

"See you bright and early," said Dennis. "I love you." Then it was his turn to hug Jack.

"I love you guys, too," said Jack, tears beginning to well in his eyes. "Thanks for doing this. I really mean it."

"It's fine," I said. "Good luck getting settled, and be safe."

"Don't worry, Mom."

Dennis and I climbed back in the car and headed home, both of us fighting tears.

"God, he's brave," said Dennis. We rehashed the way he had told Colby what was going on—still without saying the word *cancer*—and then we giggled about Colby's haircut comment.

Sometimes, you just had to laugh at stuff. Otherwise, you couldn't make it.

* * *

For almost the next forty-eight hours, I worried about Jack.

On Monday, Dennis rose at 5:30, threw on some clothes, and got on the road to Athens. Traffic probably wouldn't be an issue at this hour, especially heading away from Atlanta, but on the way back, it could be a problem.

"I'll be ready when you get here," I said.

They arrived around 8:15 and I jumped in the car, where Jack was sleeping in the back seat. Dennis went to get ready for work and I started driving to Emory. We arrived there shortly before nine. Twenty minutes later, we were on I-85 north, and we pulled into the apartment complex parking lot at 10:45.

"I'm glad you scheduled all your classes in the afternoon."

"Yeah. I've got plenty of time to get ready, and take the bus in to campus."

"See you tomorrow, honey. Four more days! That's all!"

Jack grimaced. Like me, he wasn't a morning person. "Right. Just four more days."

"Have a good day, and I'll see you tomorrow."

I got out of the car and gave him a hug, then watched my lanky son amble away. At least he didn't have to climb stairs.

Day Two was a redo, and I got home from Athens about noon. I sat down at my computer and decided to write an email that had been on my list to send. In my message to the Atlanta Street Theatre director, I told Jack's whole story, and part of what I wrote is below:

Tues Aug 17, 2010
Dear Nevaina,

I wanted to write to thank you for your work with Jack and everyone back in May and June...I have been wanting to apologize to you ever since for having to leave right away....

I just wanted to update you a little bit about Jack. As he shared with the group, he had a brain tumor. It was diagnosed on May 8, his 19th birthday, just before emergency surgery he had that night at Northside Hospital....

What he didn't share was that that first surgery did not take care of his tumor, which was still there during his time with you...Jack's dad and I took him to Duke University Hospital for a second surgery on June 30....They gave him a green light to go back to UGA this fall, which he did last Friday. However, this week is Jack's last week of radiation, so his father and I are commuting back and forth to Athens to get him in for treatment in the morning, before his afternoon classes.

It was an absolute blessing for Jack to be involved in Atlanta Street Theatre this summer, and the timing actually worked out perfectly in between his two surgeries. Jack was thrilled to be a part of your program and enjoyed every day there, while dealing emotionally with his illness. He handled everything that happened bravely and always maintained good spirits and a positive attitude. He has had some hair loss and fatigue recently, but he's grateful that he is almost done with his ordeal and that he can be back in school this fall. He has already gotten involved with organizing an improv group there!

Thanks so much for everything you said prior to the show about Jack, too. It was wonderful for our whole family to hear your compliments of Jack. I wish he could have heard them. Jack was amazingly enriched by your program. We truly enjoyed seeing him and all the kids and we think you are doing something wonderful.

Sincerely,
Julie McDermott

* * *

On Wednesday, Day Three, everything went according to plan again. On the way back to Athens, Jack told me a story about his ride in with his father.

Evidently, Chick-fil-A had gotten his order wrong at the drive-through. He always ordered a chicken, egg and cheese biscuit, and the person at the window gave him chicken nuggets instead. Jack realized it just as Dennis was about to pull out of the restaurant's parking lot.

"You know how Dad is," said Jack. "He didn't want to go back and let me get what I wanted."

"Was traffic bad? Were you guys behind schedule?"

"No! Plus, I checked the bag right away to make sure, and when I told Dad it was wrong, know what he said?"

"What?"

"*You'll live, though, right, Jack?*"

I shook my head. "So, what did you do?"

"I said, 'Dad, come on. We're not even out of the parking lot. Please drive back around, or let me go in and get it.'"

"Did he?"

"He pulled into a parking place, I went inside and told the guy it was wrong, and he gave me two!"

I laughed. "Good. Did you eat both?"

"Yep." He rolled his eyes and laughed with me. "Two more days, Mom."

I smiled. "We got this."

On Thursday, they ran into a big traffic jam on the way back to Atlanta, and Dennis called me from the road.

"I'm going to take him straight to Emory," said Dennis. "Can you meet us there, and I'll go to work?"

"Sure," I said. "On my way."

I drove Dennis' car down and pulled over near the valet. Dennis and Jack had just arrived. Dennis gave me a kiss and jumped in his car. "Traffic was horrible coming in. See you to-night."

I was glad he had some flexibility; balancing a commute to Athens with work demands wasn't easy for him. But his boss and coworkers knew about Jack now, and had sent him many messages of concern and support. "See you tonight, babe."

Jack and I took the elevator down and he checked in. Not long after, we were on our way back up to the car.

"One day more, Mom," he said, repeating a line from a high school play he had acted in, *Les Miserables*. "One day more."

* * *

The next day was Friday, August 20: Day Five, the last day of Jack's twenty-five days of radiation.

On the drive in from Athens, Jack and Dennis hadn't made a breakfast stop because Jack said he wanted to sleep. They got to our house a little earlier than usual, and I slid behind the wheel to go to Emory.

"Do we have time to go to a Chick-fil-A on the way?" he asked.

"I think so. There's one at the turn to Briarcliff, across from Starbucks."

"Good."

We got to it in plenty of time and got in the drive-through line. In a few minutes, Jack had his chicken, egg and cheese biscuit. But getting out of the parking lot and onto the busy North Druid Hills Road, stacked with traffic headed for the highway, took a few minutes. Now we'd have to make a left turn onto Briarcliff Road. I got in the turn lane and waited. I'd missed the arrow, but the light was green. It looked clear, so I started to turn.

"MOM!" yelled Jack. "STOP!"

I slammed on the brakes just as I saw a car coming. If I hadn't stopped, it might have hit us on the passenger side.

"Jack! I could have made it!" I wasn't sure of that, but it's what I said, and I was bent on making it to Emory on time.

He looked at me with a flash of anger. "No, you couldn't have, Mom! God, after all we've been through, if that car had hit us—"

"But I still think—"

"What? I saw how fast that car was coming! Didn't you?"

We sat in silence as we cycled through the light. When the green arrow appeared, I turned.

"I hope we're not late," I said.

"Who cares if we are? We didn't wreck!"

We pulled up to the valet at two minutes after nine and headed to the elevator, not speaking. When they called Jack in, I sat and read with the other caregivers and patients.

He didn't come out at the normal time, and a few minutes later, I went to ask the receptionist what was taking so long.

"Is today his last day?" she said.

"Yes," I said. "Shouldn't he be done by now?"

"I believe he is done, and Dr. Natia is meeting with him now. Do you want me to see if he wants you to come down to the room?"

"Yes, please."

I stood and waited as she called. A moment later, she hung up. "He says for you to wait out here, and he'll see you when he's done."

"How long will it be?"

"I don't know—but it may be a few minutes. After the last treatment, the doctor usually goes over everything with the patient."

I sat back down, feeling hurt and left out. Was Jack excluding me because of what had happened in the car? Was he mad at me?

Twenty minutes later, he came out to the waiting room and told me he was all done.

"Why did you want me to wait out here?"

"I just wanted to do it myself, Mom."

"Okay. I would have liked to come back there, though. Are you mad at me?"

"Well, yeah," he said. He looked into my eyes. "You're still acting like we didn't almost crash on the way over here."

I paused. "So, because of that, you didn't want me to come back to see the doctor with you? I would have liked to, since today's your last day. I feel hurt."

"Well, now you know how I felt when you didn't believe me that that car was coming and was about to hit us."

I looked down. Our near-miss on the road had really affected him, and he had taken out his feelings on me. My skill dodging a truck that other day was forgotten, and didn't matter now. But that was part of being a mom. "Fine. Ready to go?"

We walked over to the elevator in silence, took it up and went to wait for the car. Once we had buckled our seat belts, I turned to Jack. I still didn't want to admit I'd made a bad judgment on the road—I told myself that he had overreacted—but I began to realize that he'd really felt afraid, and that he was hurt, too. "I'm sorry for not believing you, and for acting like it was nothing."

"It's okay." He stared straight ahead.

"Honey, we've been through so much together. Let's not end today on a bad note, okay?"

I reached over to hug him, and he hugged me back. Then we headed for Athens. The tension between us had dissipated, and we listened to his tunes and sang on the way. When he played "All the Above," we really got into it, especially when we got to the lines about picturing yourself in the singer's place, or in our case, in Jack's place.

During the song, my eyes brimmed with tears. Jack had been through so much hell, and he really was a miracle. When it ended, we played it again and tag-teamed some of the closing lines.

I was tired from all the driving this week, but too soon, we got to his apartment, and I got out of the car to hug him again. "Well, I guess this is it."

"Thanks so much, Mom."

"Now, you be careful. Call me this weekend, and text me sometimes, okay?"

"I will. Don't worry."

* * *

That Saturday night, we had dinner with some friends we hadn't seen in months. It was a wonderful evening, and on Sunday, I spent the day relaxing. Annette and I went to see a matinee, and life felt almost normal. Jack called on Sunday night and said that all was good, and although we spoke for only a short time, I felt relieved.

On Tuesday morning, I got an email reply from Nevaina.

Tues, Aug 24, 2010

Reading your note, I was overcome with emotion on so many levels. Jack is an example of the indomitable nature of the human spirit.

I was impressed with his insight and encouraged by his disposition every day and now to know that he was dealing with all of this in the midst...I am in awe of the young man that you have raised!

He said that he did not know what he would do without his mom and I see why. I often think that God gave me the best Mom that Heaven had to offer...but I see that you could give her a run for her money on that title :)

May God strengthen you and your family, and let Jack know that I am thinking of him and am so proud of him for who he is and who he is becoming.

Nevaina

I cried as I read it, and cried more as I read it over and over again.

* * *

The rest of August flew by. Brian started classes at Georgia State and Annette started back at school. She had a follow up appointment with Dr. Williams, the plastic surgeon who had performed the procedure on her abdomen in May. She had lots of after-school activities and was also learning to drive; somehow, she had finished Drivers' Ed over the summer. She was going to be sixteen in December and planned to get her license then. When I picked her up from school now, she drove home.

Jack called a few times a week—much more often than last year—and said things were going well. He had resolved to work harder this year than the year before. He wanted to make a 4.0 this semester, and thought he could, taking only four courses. He also told me he had started going to mass on Sundays. He and his siblings had gone to church every week when they were growing up, and they went with us when they were home for vacations. However, when they were away at school, we had a kind of don't-ask-don't-tell policy: they were adults, and could—and should—decide for themselves whether to go. I'd suspected that Jack hadn't gone to mass much during his freshman year, if at all.

But he was different now: at nineteen, he had faced the possibility of death. He no longer had the attitude of invincibility that so many people his age did. He seemed to be thankful for his Catholic faith and for the many people who had prayed for him, even if they hadn't mentioned his name. He was grateful to be back at school and had set higher academic goals than ever before. He told me that he felt lucky to be there, and even said he was baffled when he overheard other kids complain about classes and homework.

He planned to stay in Athens over Labor Day weekend, unlike many students. He'd been stuck at home so much over the summer that I didn't blame him, especially now that he had moved into an apartment and wouldn't spend the weekend in an empty dorm.

His post-radiation MRI was two months away. We had scheduled it for Friday, October 29, the day UGA was closed for Fall Break. It was traditionally the weekend of the all-important Georgia-Florida football game in Jacksonville, and students took road trips to the game and the beach. But Jack wouldn't be one of them.

He had an appointment with Omni Eye Services that day, in the morning before his MRI, and on Monday, he would see Dr. Janss and find out the MRI results. I planned to take him back to Athens afterward.

I worried about him every day, and wondered if he was "hitting a wall" with fatigue. His apartment wasn't close to campus, and since he didn't have a car, he took the bus. Despite his resolve to work harder in school, I wondered if he was staying up late with his friends and partying, then feeling bad later. I wondered how he was doing wearing his cap, and how many people had made comments like the innocent one Colby had. I worried about whether his tumor was completely gone. We wouldn't know anything until he had the MRI in late October and we got the results.

I went to have coffee and lunch with friends, many of whom I hadn't seen in what felt like ages. Everyone knew about Jack now, or almost everyone. When I ran into friends at the local YMCA, they asked me how he was doing and offered kind wishes.

One Sunday morning, when Dennis got home from teaching his first grade Sunday School class, he told me that our pastor had come up to him before class and had taken him aside.

"He wasn't happy that we hadn't told him about Jack," said Dennis.

"What do you mean, 'wasn't happy?'" I asked.

"He said he had heard a rumor that someone in our family had been seriously ill. So I told him the whole story."

"And?"

"And when I was finished, he said, 'Why didn't you tell us? We could have prayed for him while he was going through all that.' I explained that Jack wanted to keep things private, that there had been a whole lot of people praying for him anyway, and that we had decided early on to let Jack drive the flow of information."

"Did he understand?"

"I don't know."

I shook my head. "You know, I get it that he would have liked to know, and that he would have liked to ask people to pray for Jack. I mean, he's our pastor, and he knows us. But wouldn't it have been nice if, after you explained why we didn't tell him, he'd have said something like, 'Oh, well, what you must have been going through,' or, 'What can I do now to help?' Like, if he'd have just understood, and respected our decision to let Jack keep it private. Isn't it okay to do that?"

"I know, Jule. But it's part of his job to gather the community to pray for one of its members. Maybe he felt slighted, or hurt."

"Maybe," I said. But the mama bear in me had taken over, and she was not going to let this one go. "I get it, that he wishes he had known, but still. Jack's feelings were our priority—no one else's."

"Well, anyway, he knows now, and so does the parish, probably. Now that Jack's at school, he won't have to face anyone here. He'll only have to face people at UGA. But he has good friends there, and it's a big place. Maybe his hair will grow in fast."

"They said it should be in by Thanksgiving, and then you won't be able to tell he ever lost it."

"Well, to a college kid, Thanksgiving is a long time away."

"I know," I said. "He wasn't thrilled that it would take *that* long."

"Did you rebook our tickets for Texas?"

I nodded. "I just hope nothing happens to keep us from going. Jack's counting on it."

Chapter 17

September 7 - November 1

And the day came when the risk to remain tight in a bud
was more painful than the risk it took to blossom.

– Anaïs Nin

The day after Labor Day, Jack sent me a photo of himself with
two of his grade school friends who had been in Athens over the
holiday weekend. They were standing in front of his apartment-
complex pool and wearing swimsuits. Jack didn't have his ball cap
on, and he had a big smile on his face.

His head wasn't just bald, it was hairless. It was also bumpy,
and you could see his scar in front. He looked like a cancer patient. I was amazed that he had allowed his picture to be taken
without his cap. Then I realized that he didn't need to be private
anymore.

He owned what had happened, and he was going public.

I wrote him back and thanked him for the photo, but I didn't ask any questions. A few days later, I sent him this email:

Sept 9, 2010
Dear Jack,

Just wanted to write a quick short note to tell you I love you.

I know you have a lot going on, and so I will resist my urge to write you a long letter. I am glad you are busy, and I know you can do everything you have to do, and you will do great at ALL of it. I am so proud of you, I cannot find the words to express how much.

Every time I go upstairs, when I walk by the open door to your bedroom, I think of you and of those nights this past summer when you were there. When you and I talked before you went to sleep. When you needed me, and I needed you. When we talked about our fears and our sadness, and about our determination and our love. When you faced uncertainty, and many very difficult emotions.

But I remember also how much we laughed. How much we sang. How much we talked about family/siblings, golf, poker, drama, friends, LOST, football, UGA, the future, etc., etc.

You kept me going. You gave me so much. I knew you loved me.

I miss those nights. I miss you a ton, but I am happy that you are happy. I think you are an absolutely wonderful, strong, kind, terrific young man, and so does dad.

I believe in you and in your strength to do all that you must do to succeed and to survive. You're a Miracle, Baby!

But you are still my baby boy.

I love you,
Mom

The next morning as I drank my coffee, I checked my email and found Jack's reply, which he'd sent at 12:30 am.

Sept. 10, 2010
Dear Mom,

First of all please do not be hesitant to write me a very long letter. I have enough time to read any emails, no matter how long they are.

Second of all, that email made me cry tears of joy. I remember all the times I cried heavily in my room and you cried with me and hugged me and we comforted each other. I could never have made it through those scary and sad nights without your comfort and advice. You are a source of strength for me. The fact that you believe in me is truly a source of strength.

You kept me going too and I do love you.
I LOVE YOU!
-Jack

* * *

Life continued without Jack at home.

Fall, my favorite season, was around the corner, and that meant football, the changing colors, and cooler temperatures—in that order. The new and recovered furniture had been delivered, and we were enjoying the room next to the kitchen, which we had uncreatively dubbed "the new room." I hung two of Dad's landscape paintings in it and filled the built-in bookshelves on either side of the tall, arched wide window. On Sunday afternoons, we watched the Atlanta Falcons play football on TV, and sometimes

Mom and Dad came over and joined us. Keegan planned to fly back down at the end of October for the weekend Jack would be home and have his appointments.

Jack and I kept in touch, but I tried not to hover. He was doing fine taking the bus in to campus, and classes were going well. He had decided to apply to the Business School and had declared a major in Finance; he had always done well in math, and wanted a more practical and marketable degree than Theatre. He was still involved in the improv group with his friend Jason, and he had met lots of new people this semester. He'd gotten into a habit of getting to classes early and staying a bit late in hopes of meeting and talking to girls.

Sometime in late September, I was sitting in the new room having a drink with Dennis before dinner when I got another message from Jack. He had forwarded me an email that he had just received from the student executive board of UGA Relay for Life, the organization that raised money for cancer research.

Subject: CONGRATS FROM RELAY SURVIVORSHIP COMMITTEE!!

Congratulations, you have been selected to be a member of UGA Relay For Life's Survivorship Committee!

We are so excited to meet you all and get the year started! Here are a few details you need to know:

* Committee Kickoff is this Tuesday, the 21st, at 7pm in Memorial Hall Ballroom
* Bring $5 to the kickoff so you can get your committee t-shirt!
* Please email us back letting us know you received this email so we can be sure we have your correct email address.

GET EXCITED!! Each and every one of you is going to help make this year's Relay bigger and better than ever! And please don't hesitate to email or call us with any questions! See you Tuesday!

Jack hadn't said a word to Dennis or me about UGA Relay for Life, or mentioned that he might try to get involved. I'd heard of Relay, but I wasn't sure exactly how it worked, and we had never made a donation. I read his email aloud to Dennis, and we marveled at how far he had come from the beginning, when he had clamped down like a turtle and we had shielded him. Now, here he was, doing things like getting his photo taken without his ball cap on, and applying to the Relay for Life Survivorship Committee. We didn't know what that would entail, but we were surprised and thrilled.

I wrote him back this response:

WOW! TERRIFIC! CONGRATS!
WE LOVE YOU
MOM AND DAD

We talked to him on the phone that weekend and asked how he found out about Relay and why he had decided to get involved. He said he had seen something about it on a Facebook newsfeed from a Relay executive board member who had gone to his high school. It said the organization was looking for cancer survivors to serve on the Survivors Committee.

Jack had gone to a dinner they held at a Mellow Mushroom in Athens to find out more. He sat down at the table with a group of about ten other students, and while they waited for their pizza, everyone introduced themselves and told their stories.

"When it was my turn," he said, "I went through everything, and then somebody asked me when it all happened. So I said, it just happened this summer, and they were like, 'What? And you're here, now?' Everyone was amazed I was back in school."

"It *is* amazing," I said.

"It's because of you and Dad, Mom. I wouldn't be here without you."

"*You* did it, though. We're so proud of you."

"We didn't take 'no' for an answer, Mom!"

* * *

On Thursday, September 23, I called my friend Ann, another of my college roommates. She, Alison and I spent our junior year in France and lived in an apartment together there. We talked for a while as I brought her up to date and explained why I hadn't been in touch before. That night, I received this email from her.

Sept. 23, 2010
Hey Julie,

It was great to talk with you today. John and I are so very sorry for the heartache and fear your family has been through in the last few months. I am so glad to know what's going on with you, because now I can pray for you and Jack and for healing and full recovery!

Thanks for letting me know what you've been dealing with. Take good care of yourself, allow others to care for you too, right now, it only makes you stronger (and if not now, when?) I'll be thinking of you, keep in touch.

Love,

Ann

* * *

The next few weeks flew. On Friday, October 22, Dennis and I drove to Athens for Parents' Weekend. We had attended it the year before, and our focus then had been on going to the activities and learning about the university. This year, we just wanted to spend time with Jack.

That evening, we picked him up at his apartment and went out to dinner at East West Bistro on Broad Street. We sat down at a table and ordered drinks.

"So tell us about Relay for Life," said Dennis.

"It's really fun," said Jack. "The people are nice, and most of them are girls."

"Great," said Dennis, smiling.

"I told some of my friends that you had gotten involved in Relay," I said. "Your friend Josh's mom said she wanted to make a donation."

"Cool. Send me her email address, and I'll follow up."

"Okay. If you want, I could send a link out to everyone we know."

"That would be great, Mom."

We went on chatting about Relay and about how school was going, and Jack was full of stories. For the three of us, together again under much happier circumstances, it was a night of celebration that he was back and that all was well.

We skipped all of the Parents' Weekend lectures and took Jack out to lunch the next day before driving home. On Monday, I got this email from him:

Hey Mom,

So I did the scavenger hunt with my committee members, had lots of fun doing that. I then came home and got an hour and a half of solid accounting studying done. I'm waking up early tomorrow morning to study Macro-econ. I feel so much better and more motivated since we talked. And I can't wait to start the week.

I just watched another LOST and.....

OH MY GOD!!!!!!!!!!!!!!

THEY BURIED NIKKI AND PAOLO ALIVE?!?!?!?!?!?!?!

First of all though, why didn't Paolo ever tell them that he had overheard the master plan from Ben, to take Jack and try to get him to do his surgery (when he was in the hatch under the yellow plane),

Jack

I was glad he had taken a little "down time" to watch an episode of *Lost*, the show that we had gotten into as a family over the summer. Lots of times, when we had talked before he went to sleep at night, we had discussed the latest episode we had seen. That had given us something to talk about instead of reality and all the bad stuff he was going through. We had even laughed at some of the things that happened in the show that were too close for comfort: when Sawyer said his father had died of a brain tumor years ago, when Desmond had to have an MRI, and even when Jack performed surgery on Ben to remove a spinal tumor.

Dennis and I weren't finished watching all the episodes either, which were out on DVD, but we planned to do that over the next few weeks. I wrote this back:

Hey,

You are not going to believe this, but somehow I missed that Paolo overheard that! And I watched that one twice! All I can say is,

1. Thanks for telling me, and
2. Now I fully realize how that episode fits into the entire plot, and
3. OMG yes they buried them alive!!!! What?!?!?!?!

And if Nikki just hadn't run out and been discovered (and thought to be dead), she could have just laid there and then the both of them would eventually have woken up - and not been buried!

Let's just say, keep watching whenever you have time, you are not going to be disappointed.

And I am so glad you got more done, but also went on the "hunt"! You know, having some difficulty maintaining your concentration while studying - at times - is part of what you are dealing with physically with your ongoing recovery. And, so is emotional variability. So don't beat yourself up or feel that you are not a good man! Just roll with it, take your time, take your breaks, and stay focused overall. You can do it, I just know it!

I love you!

mom

And later, I couldn't resist sending this follow up:

Just talked to Dad re the Paolo thing, and he said:

If Paolo had told, they would have known he was down there, and they would have asked why.

And he couldn't tell why he was down there, because he had found the diamonds, and hadn't told Nikki, and he was hiding them down there in the bathroom.

I think Nikki and Paolo had a bad relationship!

mom

* * *

On Tuesday, October 26, Brian and I met Mom and Dad for brunch at the J. Christopher's restaurant on Dresden Road, and I told them about Jack's involvement on the Survivors Committee.

"That's wonderful!" said Dad. "I'm so happy he's telling his story, and trying to help others. He's been through more than most people go through in a lifetime."

"I know," I said. "We're pleasantly surprised, and proud of him. He's coming home this weekend for Fall Break. They only get Friday off, but his MRI is that afternoon, so I'm going to pick him up that morning."

"You'll let us know the results when you get them, won't you?" asked Mom.

"Yes. But we probably won't get them until Monday. The MRI is late in the afternoon, and the doctor can't see us until Monday morning. She's going to tell us then."

Mom raised her eyebrows, a worried look settling on her face. "So you'll have to go through the whole weekend without knowing?"

"Unfortunately, yeah," I said. "He has an appointment with the eye doctor on Friday morning. Can you guys come over on Saturday to watch the Georgia-Florida game, and stay for dinner? Keegan's flying in for the weekend, and since we won't be with you for Thanksgiving, we want to have an early Thanksgiving dinner together on Saturday night."

"That sounds great," said Dad. "What can we bring?"

"Maybe some wine–I'll let you know. We're going to have a turkey dinner with all the trimmings."

"We'll be there," said Mom. "Wouldn't miss it."

On the way home, I thought about the logistics of the weekend ahead. I was anxious for Jack to see the eye doctor, because he had just called saying he was having problems reading. He had been studying a lot, and said that he was worried that he had indeed "hit a wall" with vision, not fatigue. He wasn't seeing double, but his vision was a little blurry; words sometimes ran together and "got jumbled." He seemed scared, and I was alarmed, too. I called Emory, but I was advised to take him to the eye doctor at Omni in a few days, as planned; I let him know, and he calmed down.

Then Jack called again.

"Mom, I just took a test, and I bombed it."

"Are you okay? How are your eyes?"

"Not that bad. Better, actually. I thought I had studied enough for this test. But when it was over, I wasn't finished."

"Did you ever follow up with the Disability Resource people?"

"No. I guess I should, though."

"Yes! You're already registered, and we sent in all the stuff from Duke and Emory. Go over there, or call them, will you?"

"Okay, yeah. Maybe I will. If it really means I'll get more time during tests and exams, then it's probably a good idea, after all. I'll call them right now, and call you back."

I hung up and let out a deep sigh. It was too bad that he had to mess up on this test to convince himself to do what the doctor had advised. Hopefully, he would get through to the Disability office, and he could (and would decide to) take advantage of any appropriate accommodations.

A half hour later, he called me back and said he had talked to them. They were very nice and understanding, and said they would get in touch with his professors. He would automatically be allowed 50 percent more time when taking any test. If he felt he needed help with anything else, such as note taking or even preferential seating, he just needed to let them know.

I felt relieved, but I still worried about his vision. Early Friday morning, I picked him up and took him to Omni. Dr. Day examined him briefly, but another doctor performed most of the eye tests. He showed us pictures of Jack's retinas and said his optic nerves looked healthy; there was no pressure on them. The vision problem he was having was easy to fix: he needed "prism" lens glasses for reading. The issue was connected to his recovery, and it should go away over time; when he didn't need the glasses anymore, he could discard them. The eye doctor wrote a prescription and sent us to Georgia Optometry, located just a few miles away.

An hour later, Jack had picked out frames at the optometrist office, and we walked out the door. Then we went to grab a sandwich before going to Emory for the MRI. We got there on time and everything went as before. Jack had gotten to be a pro at it.

Keegan arrived on Saturday, and we had a full house for the football game and for dinner: the six of us and my parents. Georgia lost, but it was a good game, and then we all sat down in the dining room.

Dennis cooked a turkey, stuffing, mashed potatoes and gravy, a broccoli dish, and several pies; apple was Jack's favorite, so there were two of those. My only contributions were my traditional sweet potato and marshmallow casserole (which Jack loved) and fresh cranberry sauce.

After dinner, we all walked with Mom and Dad to the front door to say goodnight. Then Dad turned to Jack.

"Listen," said Dad, "I just *know* the results you're going to get on Monday will be good. I'm sure of it."

"Thanks, Granddad. Love you."

I gave my father a look of gratitude. "I love you, Dad."

"I love you, too. We both love all of you." He looked around at everyone. "Thanks so much for having us tonight! It was fun to have our own Thanksgiving dinner, and it was absolutely delicious."

Mom echoed his sentiments, and I walked out to the front porch with Dennis to say a final goodnight and to hug them. "Thanks for coming. I'll let you know the results as soon as we get them."

"Okay," called Mom. "Goodnight."

The next morning, October 31, 2010, my home phone rang just after eight o'clock and woke me up. Dennis had already risen and was downstairs drinking coffee.

"Hello?" I said into the receiver.

"Julie! Julie!" My mom's voice was frantic.

"What's the matter?"

"Come quick! I think Dad's dead!"

* * *

I threw some clothes on, and Dennis and I raced the three miles to their house. We found an ambulance parked in front of it. I jumped out of the car and ran inside to my parents' bedroom, hoping it was a false alarm. I was wrong.

I knelt by the bed, saw my dad lying there lifeless. I shook him and pleaded with him to wake up. Mom wasn't in the room. EMS workers and my parents' neighbor Patti, a Physician's Assistant, came in and told me what had happened. Hours earlier, Dad had passed away peacefully in his sleep. When Mom woke up and found him, she freaked out, called 911, ran across the street to get Patti, and called us.

"You need to go to your mother," said Patti softly. "She needs you."

I went to the living room and found Mom in the corner, shaking and sobbing uncontrollably. Mom had met Dad when she was fifteen, and they had been married for fifty-eight years. She was in shock: life without him was unthinkable and unbearable. She kept pleading for someone to wake him up and bring him back. I wanted the same thing, but I had to help her. I was afraid she was going to have a heart attack. I held her close and tried to calm her down.

With effort, I got her to stop shaking, but her tears kept flowing. We called Bart several times and he didn't pick up. Dennis finally left for his house to try to find him, and I kept calling his number. I finally connected with him, gave him the terrible news, and then called Dennis, who turned around to come back. I called Pam, who was in California; because of the time difference, she was still in bed. I left her a frantic message, and when she called back a little later, I told her in between sobs of my own.

Pam got on the next plane to Atlanta, and that night, everyone came over to my house, including the pastor of my parents' church. Mom was inconsolable. Dad had had a pacemaker and a heart valve replacement several years ago, and since then he'd been doing fine. He had even played golf with his buddies on Friday. On Saturday night, he'd told us all a story about how he parred the last hole. Then last night, in his sleep, his heart had just given out.

In a fog, we talked about making the arrangements and writing his obituary. Dad had wanted a memorial service rather than a funeral. We had called relatives and friends all day to tell them of his passing, and Dennis told our pastor and asked for his prayers.

* * *

The next morning, I took Jack to his appointment with Dr. Janss; Dennis and Keegan went with us. On the way there, I felt numb and exhausted. The world had changed in one day again. My father was gone, and life was forever different.

I felt a deep sadness and despair. I hadn't been prepared to let him go. He'd always been there for me, and I had taken it for granted that he always would be, despite his age. I was glad I had told him I loved him and had hugged him the last time I saw him. But I wished he were still here, and that I could call him today with the MRI results.

When the nurse summoned Jack, the four of us walked to the exam room to wait for the doctor, who appeared from around a corner a moment later. She walked up behind Dennis and planted a kiss right on his cheek. He turned toward her with a baffled look on his face; he'd never met her and didn't realize she was the doctor.

"It's clean!" she said. "The MRI is clean! Jack is cancer-free!"

"Oh, thank God," I said. "Honey, this is Dr. Janss."

"Sorry if I startled you, Mr. McDermott," she said. "I just couldn't wait to give you the good news!"

"That's okay," said Dennis. "How wonderful!"

"Thank God!" said Jack, tears brimming in his eyes. He hugged me, his dad, and Keegan; soon we were doing a group hug.

"Now," said Dr. Janss, all smiles. "I'll do a quick exam. I know you're on the way back to Athens."

She did make it fast. I reminded her that Jack had a follow-up appointment with Dr. Friedman at Duke on December 21–I had already booked our flights. Per the instructions of his doctors at Duke and Emory, Jack was to have an MRI every two to three months for the next year, and he would see Dr. Janss after each; Duke wanted her to send them the results.

Dr. Janss asked Jack how things had been going at school, and he said, "Fine."

Then she asked whether he'd had a flu shot.

"No."

"I strongly suggest you get one," she said. "I can even do it today, if you want."

"No, thanks."

"Jack," I said. "Are you sure? Maybe it would be a good idea—"

"No, Mom. I don't get sick."

Dr. Janss gave me a look, then turned her eyes back to the patient. "You don't get sick, yet you had a brain tumor."

"That's different," said Jack. I thought it was a little harsh, too.

She threw up her hands. "Okay, you're an adult, and none of us can make you get one. But if you change your mind—"

"I won't."

"Come on, Jack," said Keegan. "Why not?"

Jack stared at his older brother. "I don't *need* it."

Tension hung in the air as no one spoke for a few seconds, and a new fear cropped up in my mind. Way back when, Dr. Tomaras had told us (and the doctors at Duke had confirmed) that if Jack ever started throwing up *and* didn't feel like he could stop, it could be a sign that his shunt had failed, and he needed to go to the nearest ER immediately. If he got a flu shot and then, sometime in the future, he couldn't stop throwing up, wouldn't he be better able to know that it wasn't the flu—and that he should go to the ER?

I pushed away my fear. Though I wished Jack had acquiesced about getting the shot, I sympathized with his attitude. He'd had so much done to his body, had been poked so many times and been given so few choices, that I understood his unwillingness to do what he was told, this time. I also knew he understood what to be aware of with the shunt.

Dennis spoke up. "If he changes his mind, Doctor, we'll let you know. By the way, we're all kind of shaken up today because Jack's grandfather, Julie's father, just passed away unexpectedly yesterday morning."

Dr. Janss' hand flew to her mouth. "Oh, no! I'm so sorry."

"Thank you," I said. "We saw my dad on Saturday night, when he and my mom came over for dinner. He told Jack he was sure that the results of his MRI would be good."

"Well, he was right," said Dr. Janss. "Please accept my sincere condolences."

We thanked her and said goodbye. Dennis headed to the office, and Keegan and I took Jack back to Athens. Before we started out, I called Pam to tell her the good news and asked her to let Mom know.

"I'm taking Jack back to school now, but he'll be back for the services. I'll see you at the funeral home."

Perhaps because the Aflac Cancer Center was pediatric, Dr. Janss sent this note to our pediatrician, Dr. Julius Sherwinter (though we didn't request her to), and gave me a copy:

VISIT DATE: 11/01/2010
DIAGNOSIS: Pineal germinoma
Dear Dr. Sherwinter:

It was a pleasure to see Jack and his family today for clinical and radiographic follow-up. Jack is now a 19-year-old male who was diagnosed with a pineal tumor in May 2010. He was initially seen at Peachtree Neurosurgery and a shunt was placed to relieve his obstructive hydrocephalus. He completed staging with tumor markers and imaging of the spine, and he underwent a definitive surgical resection of tumor on June 30, 2010. Surgical pathology was consistent with a malignant germinoma. He was subsequently referred to us for radiation therapy, and he received ventricular volume radiation therapy from July 20, 2010 through August 2010.

In the interval since his last clinic visit, he has been back to school, studying business. He continues to have difficulty with convergence which complicates reading. He was evaluated by Ophthalmology and they recommended prisms to help with his vision. He is fatigued, but says he is eating well, his grades are all right, and he has joined Relay for Life.

The family is under significant social stressors because Jack's maternal grandfather passed away over the weekend, and they are saddened at this unexpected loss.

MRI of the brain performed the day of his clinic visit showed no evidence of tumor recurrence. He had no evidence of obstructive hydrocephalus.

My recommendation is that he return for surveillance imaging in 3 months' time. His family will schedule his appointment to coincide with his school schedule, and I look forward to seeing him in follow-up.

The family is planning to see Dr. Friedman at Duke in December, and we will forward his laboratory studies as well as imaging to our colleagues in North Carolina.

Sincerely,
Anna Janss, MD, Ph. D.
Neuro-Oncology

Chapter 18

November 1, 2010 - April 15, 2011

You are never stronger...than when you land on the other
side of despair.

– Zadie Smith

COOPER, Joseph Randolph ("Randy") Cooper

Joseph Randolph ("Randy") Cooper passed away peacefully at
home early Sunday morning, October 31, 2010. Randy was born on
February 12, 1927 in a white frame house on the banks of the Little
River in Pulaski County in southwest Virginia. The eighth of nine
children and a 1945 graduate of Radford High School, Randy was a
World War II Veteran and served in the U.S. Naval Air Corps as an
air crewman. He graduated from Milligan College in Johnson City,
Tennessee in 1952 where he was the illustrator for the college news-
letter and yearbook. Randy is survived by his college sweetheart,
Sally Bellamy, whom he married on August 23, 1952. He is also sur-
vived by his three children, Pamela Cooper Alexander, Julia Cooper
(Dennis) McDermott and Barton Elliott (Stephanie) Cooper, and

seven grandchildren: Keegan Joseph McDermott, Brian James McDermott, John Dennis ("Jack") McDermott, Annette Julia McDermott, Kelly Prentice Cooper, Quinn Barry Cooper, and Rory Bellamy Cooper. Randy was a devoted and loving husband, father and grandfather and an enthusiastic member of the Senior Golfers Association of Atlanta. His athletic ability was only exceeded by his exceptional artistic talent. Over his lifetime, he created numerous paintings and drawings, taking inspiration from his life and family. In September 2009, the Glencoe Museum in his hometown of Radford, Virginia, honored him with a retrospective exhibit of his work, which can be seen on his website, www.randycooperartworks.com. His family welcomes you to join them for Visitation to be held at H.M. Patterson & Son, Oglethorpe Hill Chapel, 4550 Peachtree Road NE from 5:00 to 7:00 pm on Tuesday, November 2, 2010 with a reception to follow at Randy and Sally's home. Memorial Service will be held on Wednesday, November 3, 2010 at 11:00 am at Peachtree Christian Church, 1580 Peachtree St. NW at Spring St. In lieu of flowers, memorials to Peachtree Christian Church Stewardship Fund or Milligan College may be made.

- Published in The Atlanta Journal-Constitution from Nov. 1 to Nov. 2, 2010

* * *

Keegan and I dropped Jack off on campus and drove back to Atlanta. We met Mom and Pam at the funeral home, and Bart came and joined us. Dad's wishes were to be cremated, so we had to pick out an urn for his ashes. Then we got a chance to see his body for the last time.

Mom was still in shock and was weeping. Bart waited in the hall, saying he wanted to keep his last memory of Dad from the day before at his home. Pam, Keegan, Mom and I went in to see Dad's body and to say goodbye. Keegan said a prayer, asked God to give us strength and to welcome Dad into heaven.

I felt numb and almost hollow as I looked at my father for the final time. I couldn't believe he was gone. I was moving on automatic, and the reality of his passing hadn't sunk in. For the last several days, I'd been on a huge emotional roller coaster. First I was anxious when Jack reported blurry vision, then relieved and happy that all he needed were special glasses. Fear had gripped me when he'd had his MRI, but I had felt joyful and hopeful having everyone at our house on Saturday night. Hours later, I was seized by fear and shock when I rushed over to my parents' house and learned that Dad had passed. The next day, I was incredibly relieved and grateful when we found out Jack was cancer-free.

Today, I clung to my belief that somehow Dad *had* known that Jack was healthy now. I felt comforted that he'd said so, and that he had passed away peacefully. I believed that he was in heaven, where everything was always good at the same time.

The following evening, we went to the visitation at the funeral home. Lots of my parents' friends attended, many of our friends, friends of my siblings, as well as much of our relatives from Dad's large family. Dennis' sister Cathy drove down from North Carolina to attend it and the memorial service, which was to be held the next morning. After the visitation, everyone went to Mom and Dad's house for a reception.

There was a lot of food there, but I couldn't eat; nothing tasted good, and I struggled even to stay hydrated. There was permanent lump in my throat, and the tears that I'd held back for months flowed freely. Many times over the last several years, I'd briefly imagined some future day when I'd lose my father, but I had always chased the premonition away and assured myself that it wouldn't happen for several years.

It was raining hard when we arrived at Peachtree Christian Church for the memorial service on Wednesday morning. All the family members gathered in the bride's room, which was next to the sanctuary. Among them was my cousin Darlene's daughter, Hannah, in from Philadelphia; my cousin Teresa, from Tennessee;

my cousin RuthAn, from Virginia; and many other relatives from the Atlanta area.

The minister asked Keegan to lead us all in prayer. We stood in a circle and he prayed out loud. Then we exchanged hugs and walked over to the sanctuary together. I sat down between Dennis and Pam, who sat next to Mom. Bart and his wife sat on our pew, and my four children were behind us. I felt comforted seeing many of our friends in the congregation sitting with members of my parents' church, relatives, and other friends. The service was beautiful, and tears streamed down my face as we sang hymns and listened to the pastor speak. When he said that Dad had come to him during the summer, worried and torn up while his grandson Jack battled cancer, I realized how much my father had held inside over the last few months.

Because Dad was a World War II veteran, his ashes were going to be interred at the Georgia National Cemetery in Canton, Georgia, and he would receive military honors. The interment was scheduled for Friday morning. Jack and Annette went back to school and couldn't attend, but Hannah stayed in town and attended it with Mom, Pam, Bart, Keegan, Brian, Dennis, and me.

It was a brutally cold day for Atlanta in early November. The wind blew as we arrived at the cemetery and walked to a cement clearing near the columbarium where Dad's ashes would be placed. We sat down on concrete benches for the military funeral honors ceremony. The American flag was folded and presented to Mom by uniformed military, and "Taps" was played. After a few moments of silence, the person in charge asked if anyone wanted to speak.

I wanted to, but I hesitated; Mom was sobbing as others cried quietly in the freezing cold. But I felt I had to say what was in my heart. So I stood, turned around to face the small group, paused, and said, "I remember asking Dad something last summer, when I felt overwhelmed with what was going on with Jack.

I said, 'Dad, why can't everything be good in life, at the same time?' And he said, 'Honey, that's not life. That's called heaven.'"

I turned and sat down. No one else spoke, and a few minutes later, Mom carried the urn containing Dad's ashes the ten yards over to the columbarium, with Pam and me walking on either side of her. After she placed it inside, a cemetery worker sealed it with a blank marker. It would be engraved with his name, dates, and military information a few days later. We said silent prayers and hugged one another. Afterward, we drove back to Atlanta. Dennis went to the office, and the rest of us went to eat lunch at a local restaurant. That afternoon, Keegan and Hannah left for the airport and took their flights home.

That night, I collapsed in bed. Pam was staying with Mom and would be leaving in the morning, a Saturday. Dennis and I had previously bought tickets for the Georgia football game against Idaho State. Early in the week, we had persuaded Mom to go to it with us; I didn't want to leave her by herself, and she said she didn't want to be alone. We picked her up, drove to Athens, and braved the cold and the wind as we climbed to our seats. Jack was in the student section, but he joined us for the second half. Mom loved football, and I was glad to be with her and have the chance to temporarily distract her from her grief. At the end of the game, Dennis took a picture of her, Jack, and me; Jack wore his UGA ball cap.

His hair had started coming in, and it was the last time I saw him wearing a cap.

* * *

Life continued.

I called Mom or saw her every day, and talked to Jack often. Our trip to Texas for Thanksgiving was coming up, and Dennis and I invited Mom to go with us. She was friendly with Dennis' mom Mary, and she knew several other members of the large family, most of whom would be there. Thanksgiving was Dad's favorite holiday, and I was glad when Mom agreed to travel with us and spend it together.

It was a wonderful long weekend with the family. Everyone offered their condolences to Mom and to all of us, and they welcomed her with open arms. Somehow, we made it through the holiday meal and football games on television. My focus was totally on Mom and on helping her through her grief.

On the plane on the way home, Jack sat next to me in a row apart from Mom and the rest of our family. After we took off, he asked me if we could talk.

"Sure. What's on your mind?"

"It's just that—well, almost no one in Texas really asked about what happened to me."

"I thought you didn't want to talk about it. I think they all thought that, too."

"I didn't, way back when. Now I'm okay with it, though. In fact, I would have preferred it."

"I don't think anyone knew that. They might have been afraid they would upset you, if they brought it up."

He shook his head slightly. "I guess you're right, since I was private about it for so long. But now, things are different. I feel really comfortable talking about it."

"Why don't you write them all an email and tell them? You could tell the whole story, if you want. I'm sure they'd be happy to know it."

"Really?"

"Yeah. They love you, Jack. They all really care about you. You know that."

"A few people did ask me questions, so I think I will write an email, and explain everything."

"Good. Let me know when you do, and if you hear back from anyone, okay?"

We got home safely, and before I took him back to Athens on Sunday, he showed me the email he had sent to all the McDermott relatives. It was a long message, detailing everything that had happened, from the beginning. I felt relieved that he wanted to tell them, and that he seemed to understand why most had been hesitant to ask him about it in person.

This was his final paragraph:

Obviously this was a very trying time for our family, but I wanted to share it with you all so you can have a full understanding of what I went through this summer. This is not a story of pity, but rather one of triumph over cancer. There were many things that got me through this tough situation. Some of them included the unflappable support from my parents, especially my wonderful mother, support from friends, and also the support I got from you all, as demonstrated from your terrific card, which you all signed.

-Jack

He got a few responses back from some of his aunts, and showed them to me.

Hey Jack,

Thanks for sharing your story. I know from personal experience how scary surgery can be. I will never forget how scared I was when I was diagnosed with breast cancer at 30 years old and had surgery. Like you, I didn't want to talk about it until it was over. We are all so happy that you have had a complete recovery and are doing so well!

It was great to see you and your family for Thanksgiving!

Love ya,
Aunt Cathy

Dear Jack,

You are SO right...it IS a tremendous story and I am so happy that you shared it with me! I just want you to know that I am so proud of you for being so strong and brave throughout everything that you went through. I cannot even begin to tell you how grateful I am that you are okay! I was so excited when I first saw you at Grandma's house and we talked briefly about it but not in detail.

To be honest, I wasn't sure if you were comfortable talking about it or not so I opted for a hug and it was great!!! Now I know that you are comfortable and I wish we could have spoken about it in person. Grandma Mary kept us all very well informed through it all and there wasn't a day that went by where you were not in my thoughts and prayers. You are such a sweet, strong, brave and not to mention good looking young man and I am so proud to have you as my nephew!!!!!!!!!!!!!!

Thanks again for sharing :-)

I love you,
Aunt Peg

P.S. - That's so awesome about the acting internship. Keep it up and I bet you'll be a star to the rest of the world someday....you already are a SUPERSTAR to me!!!!!!!!!!!!!!!!!!!

* * *

A few weeks later, Jack was home from school for the holidays. Exams had gone well, and he was wearing his prism glasses whenever he read. On the last Saturday before Christmas, we threw our annual holiday party, our guests spilling into the new room from the kitchen. Jack attended the party, his short hair—darker and more wiry now—covering his head; his scars weren't visible. He talked to many of our friends, thanked them for their prayers, and told them about school and Relay.

Three days later, Dennis, Jack and I flew to Durham for his appointments with Dr. Friedman and Dr. Vredenburgh. He had just had another MRI at Emory; Duke said we could bring the disk with us. Dr. Janss had told us it was clean again, and his exams at Duke went well. The doctors were very pleased with how he was doing. I felt joyful, and thankful for all they had done to save his life. Dr. V gave me his email address, and a few days after Jack went back to school in January, I sent him a message expressing my gratitude. I asked him to share it with Dr. Friedman.

In mid-January, Jack called me and said he had been interviewed for an article in the UGA newspaper, the "Red & Black," about his involvement in Relay for Life. I looked up the article online and read it; he and two other students had told their personal stories. Below is an excerpt of what he said, my own emphasis added:

"Emotionally, I didn't think about it. Three weeks after the surgery, I had an acting internship, so I was more focused on doing something everyday. It's so much negative energy, *you can't think, why is this happening to me?*

...."[Surviving cancer] basically told me that I can do anything. I was strong and made it through that, and it's incredible. It's amazing. If I can make it through emotionally and physically and survive a deadly disease like that, I can do anything. It's made me a much harder worker, and *it said to me that there's nothing I can't do.*"

* * *

One morning, when Jack was home for a couple days, the two of us went to our favorite Waffle House for breakfast.

We sat down at a booth and looked over our menus.

"Good mornin', Jack!" said our waitress. She looked familiar. "Member me? It's Rhonda!" She tapped her name tag.

She was the waitress who had served us breakfast on May 10, 2010, two days after Jack's surgery at Northside Hospital.

"Hi, Rhonda!" said Jack. "Sure I remember you! I can't believe you remember *me!*"

"Of course I do! How could I forget you? How ya doin'? You look great!"

"Thanks. I'm doing really well. All better now."

I smiled. "He's cancer-free now, and all healed."

"That's wonderful!" she said, smiling back. "I'm *so* happy for ya! What can I getcha for breakfast, honey?"

* * *

On Friday, April 15, 2011, Dennis, Mom and I went to Athens for the UGA Relay for Life event.

We got there around six p.m., headed to the Intramural Fields, and parked in the Survivors' Families parking lot next to the entrance. Jack greeted us and took us over to a big tent where tables had been set up for a buffet dinner for the Survivors and their families. His hair had grown to its original length, and he looked handsome and healthy.

We got our plates and drinks and sat down together to eat. Friends of his stopped by to say hi and he introduced us to them.

Purple and white balloons and bouquets of flowers decorated the tables, and more balloons dotted several other tents set up on the field. Lots of UGA students and adults were streaming onto the field and walking around. Hundreds of white paper bags half-filled with sand and containing a small candle (luminaries) lined the track, and a big sound stage was set up at one end.

"I'm so glad you guys are here!" said Jack.

"We wouldn't miss it," I said. "Tell us what happens tonight. Is there an actual relay?"

"Yes. Four people are running in a relay, to carry the torch into the fields, and I'm one of them. It starts in town. A van is going to take us and drop us off at our positions. I'm the last leg—I'm going to run in to the field with the torch."

"Wow!" said Mom. "So we can wait at the entrance and watch you come in?"

"Yeah. There will be a lot of people there on either side of the track at the entrance, waiting. I'll run in on the track and over there"—he pointed to the stage—"where I'll put the torch in the stand."

"What happens then?" asked Dennis.

"Then the night starts. Somebody will give a welcome speech. There's gonna be some speakers, and later, the survivors will walk a lap around the field. Then the caregivers will."

I pointed to a big square mural next to our tent with purple and gold paint handprints all over it. "What's that?"

"That's the Wall of Hope," said Jack. "After we eat, we should go over and put our handprints on it."

"You mean, you should," I said.

"No. It's survivor and caregiver. Me and you, Mom."

A few minutes later, we finished eating and walked over to the Wall. Jack put his hand in the paint and made his handprint, then I did the same: his was purple and mine was gold. We cleaned our hands and wrote our names next to our prints. Next to their names, the survivors had written how long they had been cancer-free.

Jack wrote: "6 months."

Six months since his first clean MRI, back in October. I was struck by how cognizant he was of it. I looked over the Wall for the time periods that other survivors had written next to their handprints. I didn't see any shorter than Jack's.

"Dad and Grandma," he said to them, motioning. "Come here and let's get a photo of the four of us in front of the Wall!"

They walked over as Jack handed his iPhone to a student volunteer nearby. "Would you?" he asked.

"Sure!"

Jack stood between Dennis and me and put his arms around us. I pulled Mom into my other side, put my arm around her shoulder, and leaned on Jack as we posed in front of the Wall. I felt a mixture of joy, relief and gratitude. I had lived on hope for so long, but I'd never let myself imagine this moment: when Jack would live, and everything would be good.

After the photo, Jack bid us a temporary farewell and went to meet the other relay runners at the van. Dennis, Mom and I found a spot beside the track about halfway between the entrance and the stage, where we could watch him run in and I could take his picture.

I felt a surge of emotion as we waited. We had come so far, so very far, since the day he had turned nineteen, and in a few weeks, he would be twenty. I missed my father and knew that Mom did, too. But Jack was alive and he had survived brain cancer.

He ran in carrying the Torch of Hope high, leading a throng of UGA students running in behind him. He wore a white T-shirt with "Relay for Life" and "American Cancer Society" on a picture of a torch, and the words "TORCH OF HOPE 2011" under it, in purple.

He also wore a huge smile on his face. My heart was bursting with joy and thanksgiving.

My baby boy was well.

Epilogue

"Be like Jack!"

– UGA Relay for Life Volunteer

Monday, July 4, 2011
Dr. Friedman,

Happy 4th of July.

It has been a little over a year since you removed our son Jack's germinoma. For Julie and me, it was a year of summer radiation sessions and a year of diminishing anxiety punctuated by spasms of uncertainty around MRI results. For Jack, miraculously, it was back to a full academic year as a sophomore at UGA in the fall, being a torch bearer for the Campus Relay for Life in the Spring, and a Dean's Listing for both semesters -- a first. (I often joke that Dr. Friedman removed the slacker part of Jack's brain at the same time as the germinoma.)

Julie and I struggled through this year out of love, a love parents have and ought to have for their children. However, I have often marveled over that time at the love you and all of your colleagues at

Duke have for your art of healing. As we are too often satisfied with muddling through as parents, you and your co-workers dedicate yourselves to offering nothing less than your utmost during often trying times. Your dedication to and love for your art are an inspiration to us.

I have attached a picture taken of Jack by Julie on the anniversary of his surgery, June 30, 2011. He's a bit scruffier than last year, but is a young man full of life, enthusiasm and gratitude. More than once, he's expressed bewilderment when others complain about little things like having to go to class and study -- he seems to know just how fortunate he is to be able to do such things. Julie and I cooperated with God in bringing Jack into this world, and we are proud of him. In a very real sense, you and your colleagues, again cooperating with God, have given Jack a rebirth in that life.

We thank you, and give thanks, for your dedication to your art and for the sacrifices you have made to become the surgeon you are. We also ask God to bless you, your family, and your institution.

Sincerely,
Dennis and Julie McDermott

UGA RELAY FOR LIFE
APRIL 19, 2013

This year's UGA Relay for Life is dedicated to our Corporate Sponsorship Chair, Jack McDermott. During finals week of his freshman year, Jack noticed something was wrong with his vision and on his 19th birthday he discovered he had a brain tumor. In the months of surgeries and treatments that followed his diagnosis, Jack never slowed down and refused to allow cancer to derail his life. He finished his fight, and now it is time for us to finish ours.

*It is people like Jack who inspire and ignite passion within our exec board and the UGA community. Celebrating Jack's and the other survivors' success in his fight against cancer, remembering those who we've lost, and fighting back for a cure are all reasons why we are gathered here today. We have been working so hard all year, and tonight is when it all comes together. We invite all of you here today to join us in showing cancer that it will **never** win. This night is dedicated to Jack McDermott, we love you and we are so fortunate to have had the chance to work with someone so passionate and strong.*

VIDEOS:

Jack tells his survivor story, in 90 seconds:

http://vimeo.com/40599263

Jack's 5 minute speech at the 2013 UGA Relay for Life event:

https://www.youtube.com/watch?v=srpXL4Cd7K0#t=24

Author's Note

During the period of time covered in this book, I kept a sporadic journal and calendar. I kept the notes and medical records we were given by Omni Eye Services, Peachtree Neurosurgery, Northside Hospital, Duke University Hospital, the Preston Robert Tisch Brain Tumor Center at Duke, the Winship Cancer Institute at Emory, Children's Healthcare of Atlanta, and the Aflac Cancer Center at Egleston Hospital. I also kept the pathology reports from Duke and all of Jack's blood work results from Aflac.

I kept receipts from the Millennium Hotel in Durham, NC; receipts from restaurants in Chapel Hill and Durham; and even invoices from our contractor, decorator, and blinds and shutter company. I have a copy of the program for the June 25, 2010 performance of Atlanta Street Theatre, and I have Jack's certificate for participation as an intern in its Summer 2010 Youth Workshop and as a creator and actor in its original play. I kept emails from doctors, family members and friends. I framed the poem Jack wrote for Mother's Day, and the card that our family in Texas signed and sent to Jack.

I would like to thank the following people for their care, concern and support of Jack and of our family: Dr. Kelly Barrows; Dr. Ben Sturdy and Dr. Day of Omni Eye Services; Dr. Christopher Tomaras; Dr. Thomas O'Barr and Dr. Kathy Collier; Dr. Pat Hudgins; Dr. Jon Weingart of Johns Hopkins; Dr. Allan Friedman and Dr. James Vredenburgh of Duke; Dr. Natia Esiashvili and Dr. Anna Janss of Emory; Dr. Kelly Spetalnick of Georgia Optometry; and all of the other doctors, nurses, therapists, technicians, and staff at Northside Hospital, Duke University Hospital, the Winship Cancer Institute at Emory, and Egleston Children's Hospital.

All the Above

I am grateful to UGA Relay for Life for all that it has done for Jack, other survivors, cancer patients, those lost to the disease, and all those touched by it. I thank Relay for inspiring Jack, and for all it does to help win the fight against cancer.

Acknowledgments

This book was very difficult to write. Though I sometimes fought against it, my emotional struggle came rushing back to the surface and my tears flowed, at times unexpectedly. I drew on memories of the hardest period of my life to describe my feelings when the unthinkable happened to my son, Jack.

I am grateful to the many people who helped me in the writing of this story, especially those in my writers' group, The Writers' Circle. My colleagues offered their support while Jack was sick. Many gave me valuable feedback and encouragement as I later struggled to write the story, including Pamela Smith, Freddie McGee, Jim Huskins, Bill Hines, Gelia Dolcimascolo, Beth Horton, Ron Saint, Joe Rabianski, Garn Webb, Mona Haddad, and Jaya Kamlani. I thank Minal Kamlani for her enthusiasm and her suggestions. I'm grateful to Michael Faron for his creative focus and patience in producing a cover that captures the essence of this book. Thanks to my wonderful editor Laura Ownbey for her outstanding work and her attention to every facet of my story.

I thank my friends Elen Christopher, Susan Niles, Kathy Collier O'Barr, Suzanne Dowdall, Cathy Walker, Alison Swift, and Ann Grogan for their prayers, and for helping me hold onto hope. I thank my children Keegan, Brian, and Annette; my parents, Randy and Sally Cooper; my mother-in-law Mary McDermott; my and my husband's siblings, nieces and nephews; my Bible study group; and our community, for their love and faith. Thank you for your understanding of our need for privacy as Jack battled cancer, and for your support when we went public.

I am grateful to my husband Dennis for being my rock, for encouraging me daily, and for his unending love. Most of all, I thank my son Jack for his courage, conviction, optimism, love, and hope.

About the Author

Julia McDermott grew up in Atlanta, Georgia and earned a B.A. in Economics at the University of North Carolina at Chapel Hill. At age twenty-two she married the love of her life, worked for several years in banking and IT, and then stayed home to raise her four children. When the youngest was in middle school, she began writing, but later took time off when her son Jack was diagnosed with a brain tumor in 2010. Julia is the author of two novels, a romance and a thriller, published in 2012 and 2014. She lives in Atlanta with her husband and family.

Made in the USA
Charleston, SC
02 July 2015